# What People are Saying about
## *Dreaming of the Majors*

"Lefty" O'Neal is truly a man who loves God . . . *Dreaming of the Majors –
Living in the Bush* is a rich and valuable read for anyone who has a great life
dream, and more importantly, reflects upon how to deal with life when that
dream doesn't come true. "Lefty's" personal sports witness to his Lord is truly
a spiritual breakthrough insight. I fully endorse his book. He touches some
great themes in America's historical culture. I think the book should be in the
school systems across America."

**Frank Broyles**
Former Athletic Director and Hall of Fame
Head Football Coach for the Arkansas Razorbacks

"This book by Dick 'Lefty' O'Neal is a lovely piece of Americana. It will take
you on an ironic tour of race relations on the diamond, as Lefty becomes the
mirror image of Jackie Robinson, playing as the only white guy on a negro
league team. If this story weren't true, it would be a great novel. The fact that
it is true makes it even better. If this book doesn't convince you that we are
all one people, all God's people, nothing will."

**Larry Dierker**
Houston Astros Hall of Famer
Player, manager, and announcer

"My good friend Dick O'Neal has written a very meaningful and clever book
in *Dreaming of the Majors—Living in the Bush*. The first several chapters
could have as well been written about my life in the golf world. I particularly
enjoyed his wife's reflection on their early days of marriage and baseball. God
blessed Dick with a wonderful platform, baseball, with which to share his life
and faith journey, and he does it in a very compassionate and interesting way
throughout the book. Frankly, I was quite surprised to see how much life
Dick has lived this side of heaven. I am inspired by Dick's book, and grateful
for his labor for the kingdom."

**Bill Rogers**
PGA player of the year, 1981 British Open Champion

"Dick O'Neal's writings are those of an angel himself. He is a very humble and inspiring person, whom I have come to respect and love dearly. He is truly a family man, a baseball man, and most of all he is a child of God. His writings are a pleasure and a joy to read."

**Mike "The Hit Man" Easler**
Hitting coach for the Los Angeles Dodgers

"Lefty O'Neal has a winner in this book that will stand the test of time. Reading the book brought back fond memories I had with him at two universities. One of my wife's favorite quotes is 'Bloom where you are planted.' Lefty's book definitely shows that when the Lord is in charge you will bloom where you are planted. I know Lefty was an asset to our football programs and asked nothing in return. This book is a must read for anyone who has a dream."

**Coach Mervin Johnson**
Former assistant coach for the Arkansas Razorbacks
and former assistant head coach for
the Oklahoma Sooners

"As the Executive Director for the Center for Negro League Baseball Research, my initial contact with Dick O'Neal came from my desire to interview the only white ball player to have played in two different Negro Leagues (Gulf Coast and South Texas Negro Leagues). I soon found out his career in baseball was far more than having played in the Negro Leagues. His career in baseball has moved from being one of the best high school ball players in the South, to being scouted by the St. Louis Cardinals, to the college level, to professional baseball in the Negro Leagues, back to amateur baseball and culminating in a long career in coaching and scouting. Besides having been blessed as an excellent athlete, Dick O'Neal is an outstanding person. His story is a unique perspective of how a young player grows as a ball player and how a young man becomes a Christian to stand as an example for all of us."

**Dr. Layton Revel**
Center for Negro League Baseball Research

"My dear brother Dick O'Neal has implanted his vibrant spirit and love for athletics into a moving and insightful witness about his own sports journey and love for Christ. He shares his witness in wonderful common ways by taking the little things of competition and creating large lenses that reveal challenge, thrill, satisfaction, and joy of being in the game. Of all of the sports stories

I have heard throughout the years he has captured their essence in this brief read of his outstanding career. I found it refreshing and strengthening and confidently recommend it to others."

**Dr. H. D. McCarty**
Chaplain of the Arkansas Razorbacks, Emeritus
Brigadier General, USAF (Ret.)

"Have you ever noticed that baseball is raceless? Ageless? Timeless? Priceless? Have you ever wondered why? Then this book is for you! You need not be a lover of baseball as Dick "Lefty" O'Neal is. You need not understand the strategy of the game. You need not even know any of the teams or players of yesteryear or today! This book is about how one man with the right purpose, surrounded by the right people, can make a difference!"

**Skip Bradley**
President of the Men's Senior Baseball League of
San Antonio, Texas

"Coach O'Neal has not only touched and inspired my life through baseball but he has equally filled a lot of puzzle pieces in my own spiritual path. His story is one of hope, and it encourages all of us to pursue our dreams regardless of the obstacles that stand in our path."

**Dustin Craig**
Past pitching student and professional baseball player

"As a child I also loved the game with dreams of making it to my favorite baseball team. As we know, life does have a way of changing even the best-laid plans. Dick's story of hope and doing what you love and how God used it is well worth the read."

**Don Varney**
Professional inspirational speaker, Christian radio talk show host, and
member of the executive board of FCA,
San Antonio, Texas

"Lefty's book was an inspiration and definitely shows that you can get strength from heavenly hormones rather than steroids. It is a must read!"

**Gary Delaune**
Feature sports announcer and writer in San Antonio, Texas

## Dreaming of the Majors
# Living in the Bush

# DREAMING OF THE MAJORS
# LIVING IN THE BUSH

*A Life's Journey through
the Negro League with
His Guardian Angels*

DICK "LEFTY" O'NEAL

REDEMPTION ◆ PRESS

Published by Redemption Press, PO Box 427, Enumclaw, WA 98022

Unless otherwise noted, all Scriptures are taken from the *Holman Christian Standard Bible*®, copyright © 1999, 2000, 2002, 2003 by Holman Bible Publishers. Used by permission.

ISBN 13 (Print): 978-1-63232-244-9
ISBN 13 (eBook): 978-1-63232-245-6
Library of Congress Catalog Card Number: 2008904069

Without the financial assistance from the following individuals my story may not have been published. God bless you all!

Mr. Lane Mitchell

Mr. and Mrs. Tom Power

Mr. Dick Evans

The family of Jacob and Tyler Johnson

Mr. Glenn Grossenbacher

Mrs. Margaret Ballenger Cluck and

grandson Jonathan Cluck, Jr.

Carsen Bernard

The family of Dustin Craig

The family of Sam Cordero Jr.

The family of Matt and Josh Fox

The family of Mathew Rodriquez

Rob and Nick Plancich

Bill and Debra Ehrhardt

Bill and Betty Howard

# CONTENTS

# ACKNOWLEDGMENTS

MANY, MANY THANKS to the following individuals:
 Amy and Richard Adam, my children,
 Harriett, my wife, for putting up with me for forty-plus years,

My family—Adam, Harriett, Elliott, Amy, and me

my parents, who backed me in everything I tried to accomplish, my big brother Gary, who will always be my best friend.

Gary, Mom, Dad, and me in the seventies

My Lord and Savior Jesus Christ, who has been with me every step of the way; and all of His guardian angels and Christian brothers and sisters He sent my way when I needed them the most. I feel He has always been saying to me, "A man who can lead a soul to Me is playing in life's major league."

And to all of the young-at-heart old-timers who are still reliving their lives in baseball, either by watching or playing the game: Never forget your past, because it could become a rich part of your future.

To all of you who were, and still are, a part of my journey in life, thank you, and may God bless you for making my life worth living.

# INTRODUCTION

I'VE OFTEN WONDERED what my life would have been like if someone had shared a book like this with me when I was young.

Those stars who made it to the top usually wrote the sports books. They became the household names. They tell the story, "If you try hard enough you will get to the top." As Americans we like this scenario.

Looking back on my life, however, I wondered what "get to the top" meant if you didn't make it.

Most of the baseball kids in my time grew up expecting to make it to the big leagues someday, because all the books told us we could. We dreamed, we worked hard, but for one reason or another, a lot of us never made it to the majors. I thank God I had the chance to try. Ask anyone with a passion for sports, and he or she will say the same thing.

At age five I dreamed of playing baseball. My parents wanted me to succeed. Coaches helped me to develop my talent. I pitched whenever I could. I played Little League, Pony League, American Legion, college, and professional Bush League baseball at a lot of interesting places and was even a top prospect for the St. Louis Cardinals in 1967, in the early years of the professional baseball June draft.

This is my story. My hope and prayer is that you will make it all the way to the top in whatever you are going for—and remember who helped you along the way. In my case I had to realize that there is more to life than baseball, but baseball gave me a great opportunity to share how it helped me with my walk as a Christian. It still holds a special place in my heart. But if you only make it as far as I did, perhaps you may learn a little bit about yourself and life as you go. Whatever lessons I learned in sports, particularly baseball, I used in my life as a Christian.

If part or all of your life is spent in the "bush," make it an enjoyable time. In my life the bush was the Negro Leagues. In your case it might be the position you had to settle for because you weren't able to get that top job you wanted. Just remember, the Lord has a reason for putting you where you are, and He'll be with you no matter where your path may take you. Believing in Him and following His lead will give you a life that will last well beyond this short time we have on earth.

# FOREWORD
## HARRIETT O'NEAL

*To sum up, each one of you is to love his wife as himself, and the wife is to respect her husband.*

—Ephesians 5:33

LIVING WITH AN athlete can be very trying, unless you love the sport as much as the athlete does, and I definitely didn't. Let's face it: baseball can be very boring, especially when there are just a few hits. So it's not difficult to imagine how our conversations went when Dick was so excited that he hadn't allowed very many hits. (He does admit now that even he has a hard time watching baseball with the same enthusiasm as he does football and basketball.)

When I met Dick in college, I always enjoyed watching him play, but I went to see him pitch, not to watch a baseball game. If he wasn't pitching, I didn't have a clue who was winning, and I really didn't care. Of course, to him, it didn't matter if he was pitching. The most important thing was that he was a part of the game, even if it meant playing a support role on the bench.

Just before our wedding, Dick took an Air Force job that would allow him to play baseball for them. I thought once we were married I would be able to change his desire to play all the time. I was wrong.

After two short weeks of marriage, I thought about going back home to my parents, because baseball always had to come first. Of course, Dick had told me up front that baseball was first, and I would be second—until he had to hang up his cleats. I thought he was kidding. Again, I was wrong, at least for the first five years of our marriage.

My favorite story that sets the stage for what I experienced during the first part of our lives together as husband and wife shows how dedicated Dick was to his game.

I had just finished turning our tiny mobile home into a cute, cozy home for two.

We went to church on Sunday, as usual, at Keesler Air Force Base, and I left a chicken cooking in the oven so Dick could eat before he went to his game. We did not know that the oven's thermostat didn't work, and 250 degrees was really 500 degrees. I jokingly told the preacher we had to hurry home because my chicken was probably burning.

When we approached the mobile home we saw smoke pouring out of the windows. We ran in to find that the chicken was on fire in the gas oven.

By the time we put out the fire, soot covered every inch of every room. I was shaken by the fact that our home had almost been destroyed, but I was also really mad that I had to clean everything all over again.

Dick, however, had his mind on only one thing: the game. He went back to the bedroom, put on his uniform, and returned to the living room, where I was sitting in shock. He said, "Honey, I've got to get to the ballpark early because I'm pitching in the first game. I know you understand. When I get back, I'll help you clean the trailer."

I'll never forget watching him get on his motorcycle and drive away while I sat crying on our front porch. At that moment I felt I had to make a decision: Do I never speak to him again, call my mom and dad back in Arkansas and tell them to get my old room ready, or just ride this one out and find a way to get back at him later?

Knowing what I would do even as I weighed my options, I stood up, dried my tears, and walked back inside. I cleaned the house again—every dish, every shelf, all the curtains and linens, the carpet, the furniture, every room. (And, yes, I got the faulty thermostat fixed.)

At the end of the day, my husband waltzed in, telling me how great the games were and that he was the winning pitcher for the first one! That day I definitely learned where I fit into his plans.

We never had to worry or argue about what we wanted to do on weekends. Every Saturday and Sunday arrived preplanned: baseball games—games in some of the most unusual places, such as pastures, big backyards, overgrown cornfields in Alabama, Mississippi, Texas, and Mexico.

When Dick began playing for the Gulf Coast and South Texas "Bush" Leagues, I had another adjustment to make. In Biloxi there were other white players on his team, though it was odd being one of the only three white wives sitting in the stands. The games were fun to watch, and all of the Biloxi fans treated us like we were part of the family. They also did a great job of protecting us from any verbal abuse from the visiting fans and teams. In Texas, however, I was the only white wife at the ballpark. That alone made me uncomfortable, but that wasn't the reason I didn't come back. I was working on my master's degree at that point, so I really didn't have time to go to his games; I spent all my time studying on weekends. If not for that, I would have gone back; the home fans and Dick's teammates really took care of him, and I know they would have done the same for me.

The Spanish American League took their games too seriously for me. It just wasn't fun at the park, so I stayed away from those games as well. Still, I didn't try to stop Dick from playing in any of those leagues, because he always said to me, "If they have the guts to take a chance on me even though the leagues don't accept it very well, then I'm going to play. I have no other choice. These leagues are allowing me the chance to continue playing the game I love. I've always been taught to see just the good in people." Nevertheless, I worried about his safety. But, as we know, the Lord has a plan for everything, so I was willing to go along and trust the Lord would protect him.

After Dick was chosen to attend the University of Arkansas to work on his master's degree and earn an Air Force commission, I thought my days as a sports widow were over. Once again, I was wrong. Since baseball wasn't in the picture for about the next nineteen years, Dick found ways to get his sports fix through football at the University of Arkansas and the University of Oklahoma. He also looked for ways to keep involved in the Fellowship of Christian Athletes every time we moved to a new location. He even volunteered to be a marshal at professional golf events in Ft. Worth and San Antonio.

When we moved back to San Antonio for the final time, Dick—at the ripe young age of fifty—jumped at the opportunity to be a part of the amateur baseball league there. He tried that for four years but started realizing that he had better learn how to just watch the game. The Lord allowed another dream to come true when Dick was able to become a baseball scout, and he is still doing that today.

Once two people marry, it's for life. And if one is an athlete, the other marries the lifestyle of an athlete. I tried to love and support Dick in all of his athletic endeavors because it was so important to him and because he maintained his faith in the Lord through it all. I even joined a softball team when we first got married to see if I could learn to appreciate what he found in sports. However, I ended up with a cast on my wrist when a base runner decided to plow me over between third base and home plate. My career in sports was definitely short lived, but I think Dick appreciated my attempt. It helped him realize the need to be more involved in things I liked to do also.

We both have a love for music and the arts—as well as a mutual love for the Lord—and that's what has kept our relationship somewhat balanced all these years. We knew we had to give and take to be able to live a lifetime together; our family and our relationship with each other are the most important things to both of us. Because we've prioritized our lives this way, coupled with the fact that we love each other very much, the older we get the better life becomes. God is good!

I'm really proud of Dick for writing this book. I know it was a labor of love and a long journey to the publisher. I'm glad he felt it was important for me to share with other "significant others" who have to live with athletic "nuts" to let them know they are not alone. If we really love that nut and we allow the Lord to guide us through our short time on this earth, then life is worth living.

Be encouraged by Dick's journey, and remember that none of it would have been possible without the Lord being with him all the way. May He bless you on your journey as well.

# PART 1
# WARM-UP

*Teach a youth about the way he should go;*
*even when he is old he will not depart from it.*
—Proverbs 22:6

# Chapter 1

# MY FAMILY AND FRIENDS

*Honor your father and mother . . . that it may go well with you
and that you may have a long life in the land.*
—Ephesians 6:2–3

*How good and pleasant it is when brothers can live together!*
—Psalm 133:1

"MISTER! HEY, MISTER!" came a boy's voice from across the infield.
"Sign my ball for me?"

I looked up to see a young boy waving at me, and I heard the soft
thud of small tennis shoes racing down to the field from the stands.

"Hey, mister, will ya?"

I breathed deeply the faint smells of hot dogs and popcorn, the
scent of freshly mowed outfield. Behind the kid running toward me, I
heard the backdrop noise of the fans in the bleachers, punctuated by
the hawking cries of the vendors.

It was the San Antonio Missions Old-Timers' yearly classic, and I
was to pitch that day. I grinned at the kid and nearly teared up.

*Why would he want me to sign anything? He doesn't even know who
I am.*

Then I thought back to my childhood and saw myself doing the same thing. It didn't matter who I was; he was just looking for a ballplayer who was nice enough to sign something.

I said to him, "You bet, and don't lose faith, kid. Don't ever lose faith, because when you stop believing in the game, it will cease to exist."

He held a brand-new ball and had a smile that was contagious. You can see the face of God in the innocence of a child so well. He looked eight to nine, but tall. He wore a fairly new Missions cap, baggy jeans, and looped through his belt hung an aged and well-oiled fielder's glove. Likely it had been his father's.

With a grin the kid said, "Thanks, mister," and he ran back to his family and friends.

After that experience I signed anything the kids wanted signed. Just keep your innocence and your love for the game. Don't ever forget these soft summer days with the breeze blowing small bits of litter toward the back fence or the feel of the rosin bag in your hand. We are here because we love the game, and when you're hooked, really addicted, it doesn't matter if it's the World Series, a bunch of neighborhood kids out in the back lot, or even the Old-Timers' Classic.

I felt just plain good and happy knowing I would be on the mound that day, pitching against some formidable sticks. These guys may have retired from pro ball, but they could still hit. And many, like me, were still actively involved in the game. Others run farm clubs or coach at the college or professional level.

That old-timers' game is as clear to me today as it was when it took place in 1994. But I never would have stood on that pitcher's mound if not for the people and circumstances the Lord brought into my life that prepared and shaped me for that moment. For years, I was scrutinized, observed, coached, and primed for a place in the Major Leagues, yet I never made it out of the Bush Leagues. So why don't I feel like a failure? I loved the game itself, but I loved more how it brought fathers, mothers, children, friends, and even strangers (like you and me) closer together.

My life has been anything but that of a typical athlete. When I was young I was physically large for my age and wore thick-rimmed, black glasses with heavy prescription lenses, giving opponents and fans ample opportunity to make cracks like "Four eyes" and "Fatso." And when it came to picking teams and positions, I was always picked last and I could count on playing right field or bench warmer. In school I spent as much time on stage or playing in the band as I did on the mound. That also brought on the "sissy" comments.

I'm not a Renaissance man, but my father and mother taught me the true meaning of the dictum, "If it's worth doing, it's worth doing well." Dad also said, "Someday when you're old, and you find yourself sitting in a rocking chair on your front porch, don't let any "what ifs" cross your lips. There should be no regrets." So I tried everything I could and gave every attempt my best effort.

My brother, Gary, who is four years older than I am, was one of those big brothers who took me along on some of his teenage outings. Even though I was probably a pest, I think he really liked me, and I was proud to be his little brother.

My dad never finished high school. But he greatly appreciated the value of education and taught me to never count on having a career in the pros.

"Get an education," he said, "and learn other skills so you won't have to sling a pick and a shovel for the rest of your life."

Dad served in the army and then worked for the soil conservation service for more than forty years. He spent grueling hours in the field, but I don't recall him ever complaining. He always made time for my mom, my brother, and certainly for me.

When my dad realized I wanted to be a professional athlete at such an early age, he started throwing the ball with me whenever I asked. Unfortunately for him, that was nearly every day from 1955 to 1967. He knew, too, that when I turned nine and started pitching, I would be better accepted by my peers because I was left-handed.

Though he was tired after a long day at work, he would unhesitatingly play catch with me and talk. I used an exposed tree root for a pitcher's rubber, and threw down-slope to him so he could catch without having to get into a classical catcher's squat. (To this day, grass will not grow where we stood.) And we'd talk. Talk about his day. Pitch. Talk about my grades. Pitch. As I got older, we even talked about girls. And then I would pitch. The rhythmic cadence of our conversation punctuated by the sweet slap of the ball in his glove is something I still think about daily. He taught me to take my time, think of the consequences of every pitch, and then throw like my life depended on it. I took so much time in between my pitches that it seemed to make the batters mad, but it worked. Perhaps that hypnotic pace is why one of my baseball nicknames was "Mother McNeal."

Mom said it was a very sad day in Dad's life when I had to get a catcher to catch for me because I was getting too fast for him to see the ball. Mom told me Dad would come in from our sessions and secretly soak his hand so he could keep catching. She asked me to, as diplomatically as possible, get him to give it up and invite him to become my personal baseball coach while someone else caught for me.

As I recall, I said something like, "Dad, I have really appreciated your help with catching, but I really need someone on the mound to teach me the finer points of the game." Since my dad was never a pitcher, I didn't know exactly what he might have to teach me, but it was important to me to have him nearby, and it was important to him to be needed.

Mom really liked Little League, but as I got older it became difficult for her to listen to the verbal abuse being thrown my way from the visiting teams and fans—and sometimes my own fans if we weren't winning. She couldn't stand to hear negative comments about her baby. She still feels that her staying away from most of my American Legion games over a three-year period brought all of my success and eventual interest from professional baseball scouts. She never understood that the pitcher was the center of the action and bad-mouthing the pitcher was just part of the game.

Family values work. I could never put in one little book everything my dad and mom taught me. They sacrificed so much for my brother and me. Their world centered around our needs first, and they were my first look at what a Christian should be like.

In baseball, I quickly learned how agents and scouts would talk and talk, promise everything, and, to some prospects, deliver next to nothing. Without a solid family or foundation of friendships, a promising young athlete can get lost in the machine, and many do. But with a supportive family structure, a young jock can walk on and off the field knowing he or she is loved and accepted no matter how he or she performs.

At my pitching clinics I try to teach kids to do their very best, but have fun. When the fun, faith, and desire to do your very best are gone, you may as well hang up your cleats. I sometimes see young guys so pressured by their parents to perform that their throwing arms are ruined by the time they're teenagers. I want to take those kids out to the field and remind them that baseball is a game. Feel the breeze blowing in from the outfield. Remember what it's like to react snake-like to a hot grounder, throw with your entire body, and nail that dude at first.

I distinctly remember when I finally realized I would never be a pitcher in the Cardinal organization. I was devastated. But because of the way I was raised, I knew I could keep my love of the sport, remain active in it, get on with my life, and see what God had in store for me along the way. I realized that my love for the game was not contingent on being in the starting lineup!

# Chapter 2

# WATCHING
# MY HAT SIZE GROW

*For everyone who exalts himself will be humbled, and the one who humbles himself will be exalted.*

—Luke 14:11

## The Player's Perspective

BECAUSE I LOVED sports so much, I constantly played baseball, basketball, football, golf, and track. I didn't care for track, but I did it to keep in shape for the other sports. The more I played, the better I became, especially in baseball. Fine and well, but the better I became, the more people talked. The more they complimented me, the more I listened. The more I listened, the more I believed what I heard. Here's an example: "Have you seen the O'Neal kid throw the baseball? It's amazing how a boy that young can be so strong. He's quick and deadly. In a few years he'll be blowing away the American Legion League. And after that, who knows? He could easily turn pro. And he's a southpaw, too!"

Any child who hears words such as those is going to begin to drastically change what he thinks of himself. And as the compliments continue as he grows older, his mental picture will become more distorted and his attitude more difficult to control.

In my front yard in my Little League uniform

We worship our athletes because we love their skill. We read about them, watch them on TV, and glory in their exploits. For most of their lives, these young people have been told they're faster than fast, stronger than most mortals, and gifted with the heart of a racehorse. But no one ever tells those kids the other side of the story.

Leonard Robbins, in his Baseball Hall of Fame address, said,

> We toil for fame. We live on crusts.
> We make a name. Then we bust.

I understand this to mean that we do whatever it takes to gain the fame, regardless of the cost. Then when we finally make it, the fame is so short lived that we feel empty inside. But life without the Lord is empty, too. The only way to have a full and satisfying life and get a chance to play again (eternal life) is through believing what Christ said: "If anyone serves Me, he must follow me. Where I am, there my servant also will be. If anyone serves Me, the Father will honor him" (John 12:26). He gives us purpose and passion, making the game of sport and life worth living. He's also promised, for those who trust and follow Him, eternal life after death. What a comforting thought.

Sure, I wanted to stare down the biggest batting average in the league and make him sweat! I wanted to see the perspiration running down his face, watch him shift nervously, changing balance from one foot to the other. I could imagine doing my wind up, no balking, thank you, and feeling the air suspend. I'd sneak a serpentine slider that smacked a full inch below his bat. That is living. But when the crowds, coaches, and scouts begin idolizing any young ballplayer, things can get out of hand. Then it's time for a reality check, and mine came in the form of my family and church. In 1967 no fewer than sixteen scouts talked to me, watched me, and then disappeared into the woodwork. Not only did this challenge my self-esteem, it confused me. Was I good enough, or wasn't I?

The one positive experience I recall was with a scout from the St. Louis Cardinals by the name of Jack McMahan. Jack was there year after year, talking with me and keeping my dreams alive. He understood so well my profound desire to play professional baseball.

Mr. McMahan invited me to Little Rock, Arkansas, where the St. Louis Cardinals AA farm team, known as the Arkansas Travelers, played. I was to be the guest of Carl Sawatski. Carl was the general manager of the team and later became the Texas League president. However, I remembered him as a catcher for the Cardinals back in the fifties. Verne Rapp was the manager of the team and Dick Hughes was the pitching coach. These men were also well known in Cardinals history, and here they were talking to me! This was the "field of dreams" for a seventeen-year-old hotshot who figured he was destined for fame and glory. My self-esteem was supremely buzzed, and I had never felt happier in my young life. However, working out for my heroes gave me a sense of equality and acceptance that became extremely misleading.

They allowed me to throw batting practice, and I will never forget Coach Hughes telling me to just throw strikes; this was an exercise for the batters and not for me. I heard his words and understood what he said, but my self-esteem went into hyper-drive, and I thought, *These players haven't seen me throw yet. They're going to find out why I was 32-2 over the last three years. I'm throwing everything I've got.*

Just before I threw my first pitch, I looked up into the empty stands to find my dad; I needed to see his smile before I pitched. Once I got that reassuring smile, I let her rip with a fastball. Next thing I remember is the ball hitting a red brick building over the left field wall.

"Lucky hit," I said. "That won't happen again. I'll show him my patented curve ball. No one can hit that one."

Over the left field wall again! I think it hit just a few bricks away from the last one, because I thought I could see the dent the last one had left in the building. To make a long, humiliating story short, the next eight pitches went over the fence! For all I know they still might be in flight. I didn't check because my neck was getting tired from looking up. I was so demoralized, I started looking around for someone to blame. But there wasn't anyone to blame.

Here I was, being blown away by minor leaguers. If that wasn't enough, Coach Hughes came up to me after my stellar performance and said, "O'Neal, you're the best batting practice pitcher we've had around here in a long time. I appreciated you just throwing strikes. It helps our batters a lot. I think we'll keep you around here for a while."

Either he was letting me down easy, or he was being honest and only wanted me as a batting practice pitcher. I don't know, but my self-esteem just took a nosedive. I knew at that moment that my dreams to play in the majors would remain just that—dreams!

When I left that mound it took everything I had to not break down and cry. But once I got out of the stadium and into the comfort of my dad's arms, I let the tears flow. I told Dad that after the session I just looked down in the dirt and massaged my glove. A faint breeze picked up powdered clay from the infield and frosted the toes of my cleats. My head swirled with questions, doubts, but no answers. Could I play again? Was this it for me? Was there life after baseball? I just didn't know. Maybe it was time to consider plan B (college).

At that moment the Lord spoke through my dad and said, "Your life in baseball is just beginning. Christ is going to work through you as a Christian player and coach to lead young men and women through the game of life His way."

I know now that Dad had to see how I handled humiliation before he shared this with me. I think he knew that this day would come and there had to be a lesson in it for me.

Sometimes self-esteem and peer pressure intertwine, especially when we become more concerned with what people think about us than what we think about ourselves. As any player knows, when you play well, people smile, congratulate you, and you feel on top of the world. The sun shines. The grass never looked greener, and you feel a level of bliss that no chemical substance can give you. However, when you are not at your best, the sweat runs down the inside of your uniform. The ball doesn't feel right in your hand, and you find it hard to concentrate on your game. You may feel that the people you want to please are greatly disappointed in you and are criticizing your every move. Worse yet, they may be ignoring you. All of these feelings are natural. Any batter who has not been in top form knows the disorienting and gut-wrenching feeling of sitting in the dugout, adrenaline pumping, and dreading the order of lineup. If you strike out, the feeling remains or worsens. However, if you get on base, the entire world explodes in applause, the sun shines on the infield, and the grass never looked greener! That thick, dry feeling in your gut is replaced by sheer exhilaration. Once again, you can hear the popcorn vendors hawking and smell hot dogs, and as you lead from first base you send mental signals to your follow-up batter: "Your turn now; drive me to second." And you feel like you're back in the game.

There's a danger in allowing our circumstances, our performance, and other people's opinions to control our self-image, however. What happens when we suddenly realize we used to be fast, strong, practically immortal, but now we're past our prime? Nineteen- and twenty-year-olds coming up behind us are better than we ever dreamed of being. Where is our self-image at that point? Well, if we've based it on others' opinions or our physical skills, we might be in trouble. However, if we've based it on what God says about us—that we're valuable simply because He made us and we belong to Him—we'll see that our time hasn't been wasted and that even though we may not have the physical prowess of a young adult, we still have much to offer. In my own case, I've been given the opportunity to teach young athletes how to throw the baseball properly so they don't wreck their arms before they get their driver's license. More importantly, I've been able to teach the kids something about life in general. A few of those kids have made it to the pros, but when asked what's really important, they all know that He is the real answer. And I am proud to have had a small part in their lives, reinforcing that truth.

In retrospect, I know I've never failed at anything I've attempted in obedience to the Lord and His Word. In His mind, success comes when we obey; failure comes when we refuse to follow His plan. And His Son Jesus Christ is a bold example of a person who obeyed perfectly, even when others thought He was wrong—or even crazy!

## The Player/Coach Relationship

We've looked at the player side of dealing with self-image and peer pressure. Now let's look at how those things connect to the coaching world. A natural extension of an athlete's career is to become a coach.

What I have learned as both a player and coach is that young athletes need to be emotionally rewarded no matter what their level of skill. It is, after all, only a game. When players do the best they can on the day of the game and feel good about it, then the coach has done an excellent job.

A good coach can, and does, pressure a player when necessary and as a result will help the athlete achieve his or her best possible performance. A poor coach, on the other hand, doesn't know when to stop pushing his players and can do great damage—mentally, emotionally, and physically. As a player, I've experienced and observed both types of coaches.

When I was in Pony League, our coach was the father of one of the pitchers. He was always on his son's back, more than anyone else, and pushed his son into throwing as hard as he could without teaching him how to do it properly. When that wasn't enough, he also told his son to develop a curveball. At the time we were barely teenagers, and my dad had told me not to throw a curveball until I was at least sixteen and had been properly instructed. He had heard that if the curveball was taught improperly to someone under the age of sixteen, the player's immature muscles would not be able to handle the strain on the arm. And that's exactly what happened—the boy was out of baseball by the age of thirteen because he had ruined his arm. He couldn't even raise his arm above his head, so he was out of basketball too. I'm sure that coach never meant to harm his son, but he sacrificed the boy's athletic future just to win a few games.

One other type of coach is the parent who's coaching, not because he loves to coach, but to be sure his child gets to play. Because of past experiences with my son's coaches, I had told him I wouldn't ever coach one of his teams.

However, in his last year of Little League, he asked me to coach, and I agreed. I determined I would learn to love all my players equally and give them all a chance to play. As a result, even though it was tough at first for Adam to not have the benefit of all my attention, the two of us became closer.

What did I learn from this situation? If your child wants you to get involved, then do it. How you handle the task past that point directly relates to how much you love the kids. My best advice comes from a wristband still worn on the Christian athlete's wrist today. It simply reads "WWJD"—What Would Jesus Do?

I experienced what Christ wouldn't do as a coach my senior year in high school. That year I fell prey to an "old school" coaching style as a basketball player. Our school was primarily a football school, and up to that year we had played basketball as an off-season sport to stay in shape for football. Our basketball coaches were really football coaches who had to pick a secondary sport to coach. If they had any personal background in the sport it was a plus, but if they didn't, they could still volunteer for the job, and that was good enough.

My senior year, however, the school board decided to change the program. They hired a genuine basketball coach with a proven record of winning. I can only imagine that the board had visions of packed stands, fans singing the school song along with the band, and a top-notch basketball team on its way to the state finals. Since the new coach felt pressured to prove his worth to the school, he put in extra effort.

Unfortunately, that pressure rolled downhill to the team, and since I was one of the three seniors on the squad, he chose to make me an example for the rest. I became his co-captain with a bull's-eye on my shirt. When anyone was caught not giving one hundred percent (by his standards), he took it out on the O'Neal kid. At least that's how it seemed to me.

Those were the days when a coach could use the whistle strap—or anything else for that matter—on his players just to make his corrective point. For those readers too young to remember that barbaric practice, it went something like this. A coach's whistle hangs from a lanyard around his neck. The coach should communicate to his team during practice by blowing the whistle to stop the drill so he can speak to the team, or by using quick, sharp blasts to point out a line fault or a foul. That's all a whistle should be used for!

My coach, however, used his whistle differently. He would stop practice, then remove the strap from around his neck and emphasize his displeasure with a particular play by whipping the player smartly around the thighs until he felt he had made his point. To my knowledge no one ever suffered serious physical injury from this, but it would certainly constitute physical and emotional abuse by today's standards. Today, if high school coaches were caught doing such a thing, they would not only be fired but also be brought up on criminal charges.

For me, the strap hurt tremendously, but the real damage was the humiliation. To be whipped and yelled at in front of my peers instilled fear in me more than anything else. After awhile, we players turned into something like trained animals, running plays on court to avoid pain rather than to excel at the sport.

The real irony was that the coach would stop a good-natured towel-snapping fight in the locker room to prevent anyone from getting hurt, then turn around and whip the team on court at practice, raising welts on our legs and embarrassing us in front of our teammates.

I came home several times with whistle strap marks on my legs, but I never told Dad about it, out of sheer shame and concern that the coach would be even worse on me if my parents got involved. It's amazing how much power a coach has. In my previous two years on the team, I had worn out only one pair of basketball shoes. In one year with this coach I wore out six pairs of shoes because I was afraid to fail him. I knew who would get the brunt of his wrath at the next practice. By mid season we had learned the true meaning of winning because we knew if we lost, it would be hell until the next game.

We won that year for the first time in our school history, and the team went on to win much more after my graduation. The basketball program experienced great success as long as that coach was there, and the teams learned to really respect him.

At the end of the season, I was named basketball player of the year in front of the entire student body. Before he presented the trophy to me, the coach talked about this great team player and what an asset the player was to the success of the program. I knew it couldn't be me. But when he said my name and gave the trophy to me, I nearly fell over. It was the first sign from him that I had done anything acceptable in his eyes as a basketball player. That entire season I had been under the impression that he was using the three seniors as competitive examples to the school board to show them that they had hired the right man for the job. He proved his point—but at what price? I often wonder how many other players he had used along the way of his winning programs.

Did I enjoy that basketball season as a highlight of my athletic career? Absolutely not! I couldn't enjoy the game because I was so afraid of failure. In baseball, his style of coaching would make no more sense than slapping or hitting an outfielder for dropping a pop fly. But I did learn some valuable coaching lessons from him. When a kid performs well, you let him know it. And if a kid messes up, you coach him through it and do it at practice, not in the game. No matter how young a player is, he knows when he screws up, and he doesn't need to hear about it in the game. If an athlete is doing his level best on any particular day, and not making repetitive errors due to attitude and laziness, then he's got the makings of a ball player. It's up to the coach to mold him into that ballplayer.

I always try to balance constructive and negative criticism. I want those kids to have good self-esteem at the end of the game, even in defeat. We can't always win, but I don't want to lose or win for the wrong reasons. I honestly believe, as golf legend Arnold Palmer, put it, "If you think you are beaten, you are. If you think you dare not, you don't. If you like to win but think you can't, it's almost certain that you won't. Life's battles don't always go to the strongest woman or man, but sooner or later, those who win are those who think they can." The coach's job is to help the athletes feel good about themselves.

I thank God for the strong values my parents instilled in me when I was young. Without them, I might well have become a very disagreeable person. My mom and dad taught me that if I was going to talk the talk, I'd better walk the walk; in fact, it was better to just walk the walk. They let me know I needed to prove myself with my skill on the field, not with my mouth after the game.

Perhaps you've already observed that the soft-spoken stars of baseball let their arms, speed, and strength do their talking for them. In my experience, that is the best strategy for keeping your self-esteem under control. It's also called humility. The best example of this type of person again is Jesus Christ. He didn't just talk the talk, He walked the walk. And even when we fail Him, He still loves us so much that He died for us.

If you are an aspiring young ball player somewhere in the progression in Little League, Pony League, or higher, you'll soon learn that at every level you will find players who are as talented as you—or better. With every hurdle you jump, your self-esteem will take a hit. And the pressure gets even more intense when you progress from high school sports into the college or professional level. Every time you jump up a notch, the odds of going further become greater. However, don't be discouraged. That's the way of the sports world, and for that matter, that's the way of the world in general. If you give your best effort at every level, you'll be able to hold your head high, and you'll never have to face those two dreaded words: "what ifs."

# PART 2
# THE GAME I LOVE

*But first seek the kingdom of God and His righteousness, and all these things will be provided for you.*

—Matthew 6:33

# Chapter 3

# THE JOURNEY TO THE BUSH BEGINS

*Humble yourselves therefore under the mighty hand of God, so that He may exalt you in due time, casting all your care upon Him, because He cares about you.*

—1 Peter 5:6–7

MY MOM ALWAYS said that during her pregnancy she knew I would be an athlete simply from the way I kicked her, wanting out of her womb.

Me at age five and Gary at age nine watching a new invention—the TV.

When I figured out what a TV was, I began watching a lot of sports and promptly decided that I would be a professional baseball player. And nobody was going to change my mind. I instantly identified with Whitey Ford of the New York Yankees and Sandy Koufax of the Los Angeles Dodgers. Since my pitching heroes were southpaws, it made perfectly good sense to me that one day my pitching stats would rival theirs. I wanted to model myself after them in every way—from their work on the mound to supporting their favorite charities. I refused to listen to or read anything negative about them. In other words, I refused to get to know them as Christian brothers; I preferred instead to keep them on heroes' pedestals.

I could just see myself removing my cap and waving to fans in the park after yet another no-hitter—the imagined cheers and applause coming from the stands urging me on and chanting my name as I walked off the field about six feet above the surface. And I would drift to sleep fantasizing that the finest sportscasters were lined up to interview me, and I would always give interviews and always sign autographs. Then would come the commercial endorsements for shaving cream and razors . . . and the other team owners offering untold thousands for a trade, but the Cards just would not let me go.

That's pretty powerful dreaming for a five-year-old kid, but it was so real to me that I could taste it. And I'm guessing that if you could take a head count of boys and men of any age, I think you would be surprised how many still drift to sleep at night imagining themselves in the World Series. The fact is you'll never have a chance at that becoming reality unless you have the dream first. Take a look at the sports world today. Some athletes today may seem, at times, to be nothing more than flamboyant millionaires, but trust me, they all started with a dream.

Dad knew early on what I wanted to be, so he began working with me. He required only one thing of me, and it went something like this: "Son, when you start a sport, and it seems too tough to continue, don't quit until you give it one full season. Give it and yourself a chance. And whatever you do, give it your best. Don't go at anything halfway. Then if you can't cut it, you can always walk away feeling good about yourself. You'll know in your heart that you gave it everything you had. You won't fault yourself, and no one will ever fault you for moving on."

That simple philosophy—the value and character trait of persever-ance instilled in me at such an early stage in my life—has been my rudder in life, and how I hope it becomes the same to my children. Though I didn't have a personal relationship with the Lord at that point in my life, He made sure I was in the hands of those who did—parents who raised me the way He wanted me raised.

Dad also reminded me that "the most valuable result of all education is the ability to make yourself do what needs to be done when it needs to be done—whether or not you want to. It is the first lesson that ought to be learned, but no matter how early a person's training begins, it is usually the last lesson a person learns thoroughly." Maybe the lightbulb didn't come on at the time he said that to me, but his statement sure played out to be true the older I got.

I spent my first two years in baseball in a small Arkansas town called Paris, and it didn't take a rocket scientist to figure out how parents and coaches wanted their teams to play. They wanted and needed us to win. But at that age, we were more interested in picking the grass, wanting to go to the bathroom, watching the butterflies—or even catching them. And most of all, we anticipated the official post-game visit to the local Dairy Queen. We didn't really want to pay attention to the ball that had just flown over our heads.

While I spent a fair amount of time thinking about ice cream, I also watched the older boys playing on the field next to ours and wondered when I would get there. Or worse, worried if I'd be good enough to get there. Would I cut it?

Looking back on my Little League days and then seeing my son go through similar experiences, I was often struck that we had the same desires and learned the game the same way. Even thirty years later, there were those kids who, once they hit the ball, wanted to run to third base instead of first and always wondered why that was a problem. Others would hit the ball and walk back to the dugout or go to the restroom. And every team had one kid who would go wherever the ball was hit, regardless of what position he was playing. Then there was the kid who took literally everything the coach said. If you told him to play first base, he would go and stand on the base and not move. Then he wondered why the coach would correct him. Those were some precious days.

In accord with my dad's earlier dictum, I persevered and did indeed make the cut. I was picked as a Paris, Arkansas, all-star my first two years in Little League and dreamed of easily and steadily advancing from league to league until I had accomplished my ultimate goal.

Thinking about it now, I'm pretty sure I made the all-stars because I was bigger than anyone else. As I mentioned, I was the brunt of all the "fatty-fatty-two-by-four" and "four-eyes" jokes and was always picked last in pick-up games. When I ran to first base, I looked like I was running in quicksand. Oh, I thought I was flying, but no one else did. When I got to play those first two years, it was usually in right field or right bench. In my mind, however, I was an all-star with a destiny, regardless of the verbal abuse I took while in a baseball uniform.

I did get better, though, and because I was left-handed they actually started letting me play first base too. Even then, people still teased and labeled me, which affected my self-esteem and feelings of worth. I wanted to be so good that people would take notice and accept me. I just didn't know the difference between pleasing myself and pleasing others. I thought they were one and the same. Fortunately, my parents had taught me I had to feel good about myself first, that God had made me a unique individual and expected good things from me that would bring glory to Him.

In my third year, my family moved to Morrilton, Arkansas. Even though it was a bit bigger than Paris, everyone still knew everyone else.

The move was very tough on me because it meant I couldn't finish Little League with the same kids back in Paris. It also meant I was going to have to prove myself all over again and possibly take the kidding all over again.

With only six games left, I told my dad, "I don't want to finish the season with all these strangers."

Dad, however, arranged for me to play and said, "Son, you'll be fine, and this will be a great way to meet some new friends before you start to school." He was right, as usual.

The league put me on a team that hadn't won a game that season. I assume the league officials figured I just might do the team some good, for I certainly couldn't do them any harm. To them, I wasn't a risk.

I will never forget showing up that first day of practice. There I was, a kid bigger than most others my age and seemingly growing larger by the minute. No one seemed to care about the last-minute addition to the league's worst team. The next time I saw a team of comparable quality was when I watched the movie *The Bad News Bears*.

To the best of my memory, I played just about every position for the next five games except catcher and pitcher. Why not catcher? The glove was so expensive for left-handers that we didn't have one. Why not pitcher? I had never pitched before, so the coach didn't want to take a chance on me. I think another reason I didn't pitch was because that position seemed to be reserved for the coach's sons.

After watching them pitch I could see why we didn't win. Batters stepped up to the plate with every intention of hitting the ball, but there's just no way to get a hit until the ball finds its way across the plate. Don't get me wrong; there were other pitchers on the team, but they also had the same problem: they were strike-zone challenged. The games seemed to last forever.

I also wondered for the first time in my life why we spent so much time and energy on fielding, running, hitting, and catching the ball, but hardly any time on how to throw the ball. My coaches always said, "Just throw the ball as hard as you can." No wonder so many kids—then and now—have to quit baseball before they become teenagers. Their arms are, as we say, "thrown away."

It took a long time for the coaches to think about putting someone other than a blood relative on the mound. And I was definitely last on the list. I had played every position, but I was too slow to play infield well enough and too blind to find the ball in the outfield. Out of options, someone finally sacrificed his next of kin and let me pitch the last game. I struck out sixteen batters, and won the only game of the season. Why? Because I was the only kid who could find the strike zone enough so the batters could swing. Not only that, I was so much bigger than most of the kids out there, my size scared the batters to death. What if I hit them? I think in some cases they swung just to protect themselves. But because Dad and I had already been throwing the ball at home for several years, I had a bit of an edge.

Today, the Little League experience is a lot more appealing, thanks to the creation of the T-ball and coach pitch. Young kids don't have to pitch, which has removed a lot of pressure from the players and made the game more fun to watch.

Finally, I was accepted by my teammates and also by coaches who used to ignore me. No longer was I called "Fatty" and "Four Eyes." Now I was the "Intimidator," and that name stuck with me for the next several years.

A new problem emerged as I started growing more up than out. I had no instruction in proper pitching mechanics, and my arm really started bothering me. I associated pitching with pain, and by the time I turned thirteen I thought I was going to have to quit my dream. I wasn't about to say no to a start as a pitcher because I knew if I didn't pitch they would put me back in right field or on the bench, which to me was far more painful than a hurting arm.

The Lord was by my side, though, and when I needed help, He was right there to provide it.

# Chapter 4

# FROM PAIN TO GAIN

*Children, obey your parents in everything, for this is pleasing in the Lord.*

—Colossians 3:20

*For everyone who asks receives, and the one who searches finds, and to the one who knocks, the door will be opened.*

—Luke 11:10

AS I ENTERED adolescence, in the eyes of my peers I was successful in baseball, but in mine I wasn't, because of my physical pain. I continued to throw hard, but my arm just kept hurting. I couldn't take it anymore.

One warm summer evening, I sat down with Dad on our front porch and finally told him my arm was hurting.

"Why didn't you tell me?" he said.

"I didn't know how you would take it. I didn't want to disappoint you."

He looked directly into my eyes and said, "You won't ever disappoint me if you give it your best. If I can get you help with your pitching so the pain goes away, do you want to keep playing the game?"

"Sure, I do!"

"I'll see what I can do," he said, and that was the end of that discussion.

Dad was able to set me up with his major league hero, Mr. Johnny Sain, who just happened to own a car dealership in Arkansas. He was home for the off-season as the pitching coach of the New York Yankees. When he had been a pitcher with the Boston Braves, most people associated his name with the saying, "Spahn and Sain, and pray for rain." They were the only two pitchers the team could depend on to win a game. He made his mark as a tremendous pitching coach after his playing days. He very graciously agreed to work with me, and I have no idea what Dad paid for the sessions, but it was worth it.

In our first meeting he sat me down and said, "O'Neal, where do you hurt?"

"My left arm hurts in my elbow, sometimes my forearm, and definitely in my shoulder."

"Let me see your baseball equipment!" he said gruffly.

Imagine a thirteen-year-old kid, about five feet nine inches, 155 pounds dripping wet looking across the table at a man who was around six feet five inches and about 230 pounds. He looked like Goliath, and I was poor little old David. I was scared!

When he collected all of my equipment he said, "You won't see any of this, including your glove and ball, for three days."

*What have I got myself into?*

For three days we did the same four exercises over and over again. I felt like I was trying out for middle linebacker for a football team.

On the fourth day, my glove and ball showed up, along with a catcher and Coach Sain—with a gun. I thought I was going to be shot! Very quickly I found out the gun was a new tool, a Jugs gun, used to test the speed of a pitcher's fastball. Boy, I was glad to learn that!

Coach Sain said, "Today we're going to do the exercises again."

*Great!* I thought, trying not to roll my eyes.

"Then we're going to warm up with the ball at a short distance, medium distance, and long distance, and then we're going to throw off the mound."

*It's about time,* I thought.

"By the way, when you pitch off of the mound you will pitch twenty-five times, and I expect all of the pitches to be strikes."

"Right!" I said to him, with all the confidence I could muster. But to myself I said, "He's got to be kidding. I've never thrown twenty-five strikes in a row—ever."

After the exercises, and the short, medium, long toss, I went to the mound and started throwing the ball to the catcher. After the first five strikes I thought, *I'm just lucky.* After the next fifteen strikes I was speechless. When I knew I had only five to go, I actually got very nervous. In other words, I started thinking too much and, as a result, threw four strikes and one ball. Twenty-four strikes out of twenty-five—not bad! I couldn't believe it. I was so excited I couldn't wait for the final day.

The next day we repeated the routine of the previous day. Again, I threw twenty-four out of twenty-five strikes. And as slow as the sessions had seemed the first three days, I could hardly believe how quickly the last two days flew by.

After I finished pitching, Coach Sain sat me down again and said, "Remind me again where your throwing arm hurt on our first day."

"My elbow, forearm, and shoulder."

"How old are you, O'Neal?"

"I'm thirteen years old."

"By the time you turn sixteen, you'll be looking at surgery! Where do you hurt now?"

"My lower back is killing me, and my legs are on fire," I said in my best moaning response.

He leaned over, looked directly into my eyes, and said, "That means you're out of shape. Welcome to your body. You have just learned to throw the ball with your body instead of solely relying on your arm."

"But when does this pain go away?"

"It depends on how many times you do the exercises without anyone telling you to. In other words, you need to start believing in this routine and doing it consistently."

This was my first time as an athlete to be introduced to a real work ethic. My father preached it in general terms, but now I was hearing it from a pro coach. I needed to get into power pitching shape.

"Oh, by the way," he said as he walked toward our car, "your fastball was much faster today than it was yesterday because your body started taking over control of the speed."

Before Coach Sain left, he gave my dad a gift for me to use once I became consistent with my fastball. It was a ball on a handle with a nail through the ball that he had invented. He called it the "spinner," and it helped its user learn the different grips and spins needed to become a better pitcher. The spinner was portable, so I carried it everywhere. I even took it to bed, testing the spins over my head while lying on my back. Have you ever heard of baseball hitters sleeping with their bats? I've roomed with a few of those weirdos in my life, and there I was doing the same thing with my spinner. From the moment I received that tool, my abilities to throw a variety of pitches took a giant leap forward.

That week dramatically and completely changed the whole way I went about playing the game of baseball. It took about three months for me to get into shape and to make the new way of pitching my personal style.

In the three years of American Legion ball that followed, I won thirty-two games and lost only two.

Word got around, and scouts began showing up in small numbers. Then in my senior year of high school, many more attended my games. Believe it or not, I really didn't care how many scouts were there. I was just so grateful to be able to throw the baseball with no pain. What a blessing given to me by Him through a man I had never met until that week. The Lord surely works in mysterious ways. My modern-day Goliath became my pitching savior!

Not only that, but Johnny Sain's instruction enabled me to stay in baseball as a coach or player all of my life. The Lord used another human being to help me stay in the sport I loved when I was young so I could share His message through sports as an adult.

As committed as I was to baseball, during this time in my life I also tried many other endeavors in addition to my favorite sport.

My parents had, shall we say, encouraged me to sing in the church choir, and I actually began to enjoy it. I fell in love with music and was the only male teenager in the choir with the exception of my brother. But when he went off to college, I was it. I started out as a tenor, but as I got older hitting those high notes became more difficult and I moved more toward baritone.

As I entered junior high school, I decided to try out for the band. I wish I could say I did so because of my love of music, but I had an ulterior motive: older-brother peer pressure. He was in high school at the time and winning all kinds of medals in music at the regional and state levels. All I heard was, "Oh, you're Gary's little brother. He was really a great trombonist in the band." I was sure if he could do it, then I could too.

Of course, since I joined the band for the wrong reason, I had to find the easiest instrument to play. The drums became my partner.

My next task was to find something Gary hadn't accomplished in the band. That quest led me to try out for drum major.

I'm leading the Junior High Band down main street, Morrilton, Arkansas.

Once I got the job, I found out I was the first male drum major the school had ever had. My jock friends couldn't believe I would do such a thing. Of course, their disapproval and taunts of "sissy" made me want to do it even more.

In my sophomore year of high school I got so tired of hearing from the jocks, "O'Neal, I dare you to try out for football, you sissy!" that I went to my parents again and asked if I could try out for football the summer before my junior year. Their answer was "Sure, but for what reason?"

I lied and said, "Well, you guys told me a long time ago not to live with regrets, so this is another thing I'd like to try before it's too late."

"OK, but remember, if you want to quit after we commit to the sport, you have to at least stay with it for one season."

"No problem. I will."

After practicing twice a day for two weeks in the hot sun, I wanted to eat those words! I found out again I was going after something for the wrong reason. It didn't take me, or the coaching staff, very long to determine that I didn't like to hit people, and I sure didn't like people hitting me, so I became a backup tight end. Let me emphasize "backup," and I was content to back up as far as I could!

Why I decided to become a punter instead of getting hit

My salvation came when the coaches met with us and asked for volunteers to be kickers—a punter and a place kicker—for the team. The lightbulb clicked on in my mind: *I can still be on the team, but if I punt I won't get hurt, so I can still play baseball!* I volunteered immediately, and I was off on a new venture.

Punting was harder than I thought it would be, but I survived my junior year as a football player. My friends in the band were very supportive, cheering for me when I ran onto the field. Gary, too, offered a helping hand. My brother had always wanted to play sports but couldn't because of asthma. When he saw that I needed help improving my punting, he practiced with me the next summer, and we worked really hard to improve my skills. You might say that my brother and my band friends were God's servants when I needed them.

I found out years later that Gary had no idea the pressure he was putting on me as his little brother. It wasn't until he and I attended our grandfather's funeral when we were in our mid- to late-twenties that we really shared what it was like growing up with each other. I told him how I wanted to excel in music because he had, and he told me he had envied my accomplishments in sports. Treatment for asthma back then wasn't very advanced, so kids who had it weren't really able to participate in sports. In fact, medical wisdom of the time advocated combating asthma by playing a musical instrument. Gary didn't choose music; it was simply a way to help him deal with his health issues. He just made the most of it. We were competing internally with each other and really didn't need to. Gary and I are closer than ever today and would do anything for each other.

Thanks to his help and my hard work the summer following my junior year, I played football as a senior to prove that I could help the team. As a result, I became the co-captain for one of the games, I was one of the escorts for homecoming, and when it came time for graduation I received offers to punt at the college level. I can thank my brother for that. Not bad for a guy going into a sport for the wrong reason. I just wanted to prove to myself, and others, that a person didn't have to fit into one specific stereotyped group to be successful in high school. The football players thought it was weird that when we went into the locker room at halftime, I would sit next to the open door and listen to my friends in the band perform their halftime show, but I didn't care.

God was gracious to me during those years. Regardless of my original intent in all of these ventures, He provided godly young men and women to encourage, coach, and motivate me. Participating in school plays boosted my self-confidence. Butting heads with a coach developed patience and showed me how not to coach when opportunities arose later in life. Serving as class president taught me valuable leadership skills. But the most important lesson I learned can be summed up by Hebrews 13:5: "Be satisfied with what you have, for He Himself has said, I will never leave you or forsake you."

# Chapter 5

# A New Definition
# of "Fun"

~⁂◉

*The LORD will protect you from all harm;*
*He will protect your life.*
*The Lord will protect your coming and going*
*both now and forever.*

—Psalm 121:7–8

HIGH SCHOOL GRADUATION brought closure to one segment of my life, but, as it does for everyone, it opened the door to a whole new world: adulthood.

Before I made any life-altering decisions, however, I first had to finish my last American Legion season in baseball. I went into the summer season undefeated, so some of the fans and scouts came out just to see if I would lose. I lost twice that summer, but one of those losses came playing against a North Little Rock, Arkansas, team who had a young first-year kid who was six-feet-five-inches tall and threw a baseball like a BB. He beat me 2-1 with his home run. To this day he hasn't let me forget it. Glen Abbott and I are still close Christian friends. He went on to play for the Oakland Athletics, moving up to the Major Leagues to take Catfish Hunter's place when Catfish became the first free agent and moved on to the New York Yankees. Glen went on to start for Oakland for four years and then was traded to the new expansion team called the Seattle Mariners, where he became their first opening-day pitcher. He played several more years professionally, but he made quite an impression on me that first night we faced each other. Even in defeat the Lord had a reason for us to meet.

After that game the scouts mobbed Glen, and I was fortunate to be the opposing pitcher, so the scouts could see me one last time. My final record for those three years was 32-2 with a 1.86 ERA. The St. Louis Cardinals' scout was still there following my progress, and we made a deal for me to work out with their AA team in Little Rock as their batting-practice pitcher, the experience of which is recorded in an earlier chapter.

Just a few weeks back from my visit with the Cardinals at Little Rock, I received news that would change my life forever. The year was 1967, and our country was at war in Vietnam. And right at the time in my life when I was so close to my ultimate dream, I received a notice in the mail from the draft board, and no, it wasn't the professional baseball draft board. I knew already I was going to be put into the June draft for professional baseball. No, this draft notice was for the US military.

At that time if a guy had a draft number in the hundreds or less, then his chances of being selected were a hundred percent. My number was six.

I found out that the only way to delay the inevitable was to go to college first. In fact, the Air Force would delay my enlistment until I graduated from college, if I signed on with them. So, since Mom and Dad wanted me to get a degree, I enrolled in the college that was most interested in me as a football player, just in case I might sign a pro contract in baseball later.

I tried out for punter for the University of Central Arkansas Bears. After two weeks of tryouts I made the team. Boy, did that news make my musician friends back home proud—and my jock doubters shocked. I could hardly believe it. Me—playing football at the college level. I was on top of the world.

Unfortunately, since I was now on my own, without Mom and Dad's help, or so I thought, I made a string of bad decisions. I had fooled a lot of people into thinking that I was a strong Christian. After all, I went to church twice every Sunday, I was the president of the church youth group, and I sang in the choir. But, boy, when I became a part of the college scene as an athlete, a lot of other fun events came along that I just had to experience. And since I was such a model high school student, I didn't think the academic schedule would be a problem.

My priorities that first semester went something like this: (1) Enjoy the perks of being a football player; (2) always have a date after every game; (3) go to every fraternity party I can, so I can be accepted in another environment on campus; (4) think about studying; and (5) go to church if I'm not too tired from partying (I was always too tired from partying). I didn't think God would mind, since, after all, He knew I believed in Him, didn't He?

Along with my shift in priorities, I tried most of the things my parents had said to stay away from: drinking, smoking, and chewing tobacco. I rationalized my behavior by telling myself I was just trying to fit in to the college scene. I had so much fun that I became academically ineligible to play spring football.

I'll never forget the meeting I had with the head coach. He called me into his office and said, "Have you seen your grades yet?"

I said, "No, sir," even though I had.

"Do you know you have to have a certain grade point average in order to continue in college sports?"

"Yes, sir."

The kicker came when he said, "Dick, you really disappoint me. You worked so hard to make the team to then throw it all away in just one semester. Either bring your grades up this spring, or you are off the team next fall."

If that wasn't enough, I received a phone call from my dad. He had just received a copy of my grades. I can still remember how that conversation went.

"Son, I just received your grades."

I jumped in. "I can explain."

"Well, explain, then."

Silence.

I had no explanation. I had simply screwed up.

It was Dad's turn to jump in. "Maybe I'll explain something to you," he said. "Looks like you had enough fun in your first semester. Well, the fun is over. Here are your two options. First, we will help you one more semester financially. If your grades improve, we will continue helping you. But if you stay on this path you are going down, then I will gladly give the Army your phone number. They've been calling here, asking for you to join their team. Any questions?"

Dad always was a man of few words, but those words hit me right between the eyes.

At that point I felt a storm of bad things had happened to me, and I recalled a phrase I had heard in Sunday school that went something like this: "Don't tell God how big your storm is; tell your storm how big your God is."

It took the next seven semesters of B grades and above to bring my marks up to a respectable level. I really paid for that first semester. But when He got involved, my priorities changed drastically and I became college student first, athlete second. Once that happened, I was on my way to real fun in college.

When I became eligible again, I decided to drop football and try out for the baseball team. I hadn't heard anything from the pros, so I assumed they weren't interested anymore. I made the team and lettered three years.

Bringing my grades up and playing baseball helped me square my priorities, but I still faced temptation, especially after I joined a fraternity my junior year. Finding a church family away from home and joining the Fellowship of Christian Athletes (FCA) helped me through those days. In fact, FCA became a lifelong involvement for me.

All these activities helped me reorient my life around the Lord, but four major events in my college years stand out as the most influential in keeping me on track.

The first event that changed my life was meeting Mr. Paul Anderson, an Olympic champion, at that time the strongest weight lifter in the world, and a man after God's heart. I was serving as president of FCA at the university at that time, and we were sponsoring Paul's visit, though

he was scheduled to speak to the entire student body. It took us a year
to get him on the schedule, but it was worth it. We couldn't find a bed
big enough for him, so I asked him if he wouldn't mind sleeping on
the floor in my room.

"I would love to sleep there," he said, without hesitation. "In fact,
the Lord needs me to stay in your room for some reason."

I thought, *Boy, am I in trouble.*

We sat in that small room together and talked and talked and talked.
Just as I started drifting to sleep, Paul boldly said, "I sense there is
something wrong in your life. If Christ were sitting here, could you look
Him in the eye and feel confident that you were going to heaven?"

Wow! I was floored. How did he know what I had been doing these
past years in college? Of course, I said, "Sure, I'm confident that I'll be
going to heaven," but it didn't take long for both of us to realize I wasn't
being honest. I was embarrassed, too. How can a man be the president
of the FCA, sing in the choir, and pray without knowing Jesus Christ
as his Savior? At that moment I realized that my faith had never made
it from my head to my heart. As a kid, I had believed in Him, but I
hadn't grown into a man who personally practiced what He teaches and
holds Him in his heart. Paul and I both saw that God had sent him to
me to change that.

We sat in the middle of the floor holding hands and praying for
most of the remaining night into the morning. But when the sun came
up I felt so refreshed; I wasn't tired at all.

This messenger from God and I went to the assembly, and when I
introduced him, I introduced him as my Christian brother forever. We
embraced and both cried in front of everyone.

He proceeded with his demonstration of his physical strength, but
he always brought the focus back to the gospel and what God had done
for Paul Anderson. Of course, I met other FCA greats who influenced
me, but Paul holds a special place in my heart as the man God used to
take my faith to the next level.

The second significant event in college that helped me realize just
how powerful He is in the whole world occurred when I was accepted
to tour with "Up With People" the summer between my sophomore
and junior years. Three Arkansans were chosen to sing for the group

in 1969, and we were all white; our state was still getting used to integration at that time. But I traveled all over our country and Canada living with just about every color and creed a person could imagine. Through music we tried to bring the world together. The experience taught me that He sees no color, as in the words to one of the group's most popular songs—"What Color Is God's Skin?" The song's whole emphasis is that everyone's the same in His sight. That song became my guide through life, and meeting so many different people from various backgrounds helped me to learn more about where I fit into the overall picture of life.

Three months into the tour, at Kitchener, Ontario, Canada, performing at a provincial fair, my life took another detour that both my parents and I were dreading. After one of the shows, the director called all the men together. He wanted to show us our draft numbers again, and give us a chance to go home if our numbers were too low to stay. The Vietnam War was really heating up! Well, I was one of several guys who had to go home. My number hadn't changed, so I was on my way to the military earlier than I thought—unless I went back home and continued college. Well, I did and I was blessed for it.

The third major event the Lord orchestrated happened in the middle of a professional baseball tryout. After my junior year I was still trying to convince myself that I wouldn't have to go to war and would sign a baseball contract before I graduated. Working out with the Arkansas Travelers during the summer wasn't enough for me. So I went to a tryout sponsored by the Cincinnati Reds between my junior and senior year just to see what other organizations thought about my chances. I was serious about impressing the scouts and really didn't want to interact with the other players and risk being distracted!

However, when I was warming up, a black guy came up to me and asked, "Can I warm up with you?"

"Sure. My name is Dick."

"Mine's Charlie. Glad to meet you."

I found out he was also trying out for pitcher, so I tried to stay away from him; I wanted to beat every pitcher out there. But he approached me every chance he got, just to be a friend.

At one point he said, "You seem to be really uptight and way too serious about this game."

"Aren't you concerned about your chances, Charlie?"

He shrugged and said, "If this game is what God wants me to play, and I have the skills the pro scouts are looking for, then it will happen. I've turned the outcome over to the Lord."

I was so impressed with his calmness that it wore off on me. I started relaxing and just having fun working out and spending time with this new Christian friend. When the tryout was over we promised to keep in touch, but we never did for some reason.

As it turned out, the scouts weren't interested in me, and I didn't know what they had told Charlie. But for the first time I learned how much fun this game should be and I quit worrying about what it was going to do for me. Up to that time I wanted to be a pro not only because I loved the sport but also for the notoriety of being a Major League ballplayer and the money that went along with it. I just never admitted it until Charlie came along. Charlie, in just a short time, helped me to understand that if I had a personal relationship with the Lord, all things would work out, maybe not on my timetable, but on His. Charlie, at that moment, became my strongest Christian influence in a baseball uniform. For a long time I would pray to Christ as though I was having a personal conversation with Him, just like I had with Charlie. It really helped me think of Him and treat Him as a personal friend.

The next year at one of our college baseball practices, one of my teammates, Roger, came up to me and said, "I understand you met my brother Charlie." Up to that point, I had never made the connection.

"Yes, I did, Roger, and we had a great time with each other at the tryout. How's he doing?"

"He passed away this week. But shortly before he died he asked me to ask you to be one of the pallbearers."

Shocked, I asked, "What happened?"

"Well, right after the tryouts, he was picked up by the Reds and went off to play pro ball. But the more he played, the weaker he felt. After he died, we found out that his kidneys had been in a process of shutting down. His body just couldn't take it. He told me to look you up and tell you that God loves you and so does he. He wanted you to be there at his funeral. Can you come?"

"Of course," I said weakly, trying to hold back my tears. "I wouldn't miss it. I have to say good-bye in my own way."

The rest of the practice passed in a blur. I could only think, *Why Charlie? Why not me? He truly loved the Lord, and he meant so much to me.*

The funeral was a celebration, not a sad event, because Charlie's family knew where he was. I could just see Charlie up there ministering to other ballplayers who had gone before him.

As I stood there over his grave, I thought, *Charlie, you showed me what being a Christian really looks like. You changed my life forever, and it doesn't matter anymore where I play the game. You helped me to just appreciate it as one more way to witness to people about His power and love.*

At that moment a calm came over me that I can't explain, and the Lord reminded me of these words from John 11:25: "I am the resurrection and the life. The one who believes in Me, even if he dies, will live." Since his death I'll always consider Charlie to be one of my special guardian angels. My family and Up With People taught me that He sees all color the same. Charlie was a young black baseball player who further proved how powerful He is.

This brings me to my final most significant event in college. I met a young and beautiful transfer student from Mississippi State College for Women in my junior year named Harriett Lee Simpson. We were in the same speech class, and the professor asked us to stand and introduce ourselves in the first session. She sat in the back of the room, and I didn't even notice her until it came time for her to speak. When she said, "Hi, I'm Harriett Simpson from Montrose, Arkansas," I, along with everyone else, turned around to look at her. Her accent was so southern, we thought we had a Scarlett O'Hara in our presence. But beyond her accent, she was beautiful! I had to have a date with her. For me, it was love at first sound and sight.

We dated off and on our junior year, but no matter who we dated, we always came back to each other. We had so much in common. We both loved music and sports (or so I thought), but more importantly, she had been raised in a Christian home.

She was studying to be a speech therapist, and I became her first subject. I had a small problem stuttering, and with her helping me, we could also see more of each other. At the same time, I reconsidered my major.

In my thinking, I was majoring in sports, but I decided it might be good to get a real degree, and speech communications seemed easy enough. I was wrong. It wasn't easy, but it did give me the confidence to get up in front of people and present what I had to say. It also allowed me to share more classes with Harriett. Harriett became my rock, and when she felt I was getting out of line she reminded me of it. The Lord truly had sent me yet another living, breathing, angel on earth who loved me unconditionally, and she is still my best friend, my lover, and my wife for more than forty-plus years.

Paul Anderson, Up With People, Charlie, and my partner for life—Harriett Simpson—all came into my life when I needed God's presence the most. They helped to ground my faith and helped me to make more godly decisions and choose His path for my life. Their influence continues to affect me each and every day.

# Chapter 6

# LOOKS ARE DECEIVING

*When I was a child, I spoke like a child, I thought like a child, I reasoned like a child. When I became a man, I put aside childish things . . . . Now these three remain: faith, hope, and love. But the greatest of these is love.*

—1 Corinthians 13:11, 13

ONCE AGAIN GRADUATION brought changes. I received what Mom and Dad had wanted for me more than a baseball career: a college degree. And now, because the Vietnam War had not ended, I had to go serve in the Air Force for four years. My Major League dream seemed to have come to an end, and I couldn't imagine life without it.

Two months after graduation, my presence was required at Lackland Air Force Base in San Antonio, Texas, for basic training. Typically, college graduates become officers, but when I chose the Air Force in my freshman year of college, the recruiter gave no guarantees how I would serve, just that I would have to serve four years upon graduation. The Air Force would check its needs at that time and then let me know. When it was time for me to serve, the Air Force was looking for pilots, navigators, doctors, or engineers for officer positions. I was blind as a bat and had a Bachelor of Science in Education degree, not a good match for officer material at the time, so I had to go, along with 5 percent of other college graduates that year, to basic training. My new goal was to graduate from basic training in order to become the lowest-ranking airman in the Air Force. This was truly a humbling experience, but I remembered what Charlie had told me: "There is a purpose for everything, and He will see that you are used to glorify Him."

I thought I would never play baseball again, but I was wrong. In my third week of basic training I was called into the first sergeant's office. I thought I was in big trouble, but all he wanted to do was to offer me a chance to become an athletic specialist for the Air Force and a player/pitching coach for one of the Air Force teams. I didn't think there was such a job in the Air Force, but this time I was pleased to be wrong. My alternative was to go to Vietnam as a radio broadcaster for the Armed Forces Radio Network.

I told the first sergeant, "Let me think about it for awhile, and I'll get back to you." I walked out of the office, turned around, came back in, and said, "You've got a deal!"

I could almost hear Christ speaking through my first sergeant saying, "You have to take this job. I have plans for you in this league."

I graduated from basic training three weeks later, in February of 1972, and was on my way to Keesler Air Force Base in Biloxi, Mississippi.

I will never forget reporting in and hearing the first words out of our young commander's mouth: "There are two rules to follow as new personnel at this location. First, do not wear your uniform off base. People in this country do not think very highly of the military right now, and they're likely to spit on you. Second, get yourself an additional job because your current pay makes you eligible for food stamps." What a great way to be introduced into the real world of the military. Life had to be better than the way it was being painted at that briefing.

Well, it became much better that summer, because Harriett and I were married. With her I could endure anything.

When I reported to my immediate boss, he told me my job was to play and coach baseball for the Keesler Air Force Base Tarpons. My office would be in the gym. Things were definitely looking up. We played college teams who were from the eastern United States during the early part of their season when it was too cold to play there. They would take a Gulf Coast swing to get away from the bad weather. In addition, we scheduled games with semiprofessional baseball teams such as the Biloxi Dodgers of the Gulf Coast Negro League. They liked to call their league the "Bush League."

I'm pitching on the mound at Keesler AFB.

When we played our first game against the Dodgers, I pitched and happened to have a good night: I struck out nine batters and threw a three-hitter. After the game the owner and coach approached me to see if I would consider signing on with them when my season was over. Since I was an athletic specialist, my commander didn't have a problem with it. I just had to make sure it didn't interfere with my military duties. He thought it would be good to show community involvement. Whatever the reason, I was glad to play, and besides, this became my off-duty employment the commander had earlier said we needed to survive.

I thought for a brief moment that I was back on the road to the majors through the Bush League, basically in an all-black league except for the Dodgers. We had a few white players on our team, and more came later after I left Biloxi. I knew they had scouts at their games.

It didn't take Christ long to reply to my thoughts. "Dick, I have put you in a league of a different color for one reason and that is to play the game and witness for Me. In other words, your goal is to bridge the gap. There shouldn't be color in baseball, only ballplayers who love the game, and with your assistance, love Me. Through baseball you are going to be a living witness of what a Christian should stand for."

*Wow, what a responsibility. I hope I'm worthy enough*, I thought. And yes, there was still prejudice in baseball, even though Jackie Robinson had crossed the color line some thirty years earlier. Initially, the other black teams didn't appreciate our presence, especially on the road. We were the only team in the league who had white players—three my first year. Our teammates and management, however, accepted us well and took care of us when we traveled. We were truly a baseball family. We got paid very little, but we loved the game.

One of the white ballplayers, Cliff Kirkland, also played college ball at Southern Mississippi. The other, Larry Smith, had caught my eye as a solid pitcher when he tried out for the Keesler Tarpons. I knew we had to have him on the Dodgers.

Once I got to know him, I found out he had played four years of college ball in Oklahoma and also that he was a strong Christian. The Lord had sent me another brother in Christ, and from that moment in time Larry Smith became known as "Smitty."

Harriett and I started our married lives in a 12 x 60-foot mobile home, and it was just right for us. Thank God she got a job as a speech therapist, which got us off the food stamp line, and life was good.

As she mentioned in her foreword, Harriett now found herself not only a wife, but the wife of an athletic nut with a buddy who was as eaten up with baseball as I was. Unfortunately for her, that meant watching a lot of baseball. Fortunately for her, there were other wives going through the same thing. Smitty married the next year, and when his wife, Beverly, moved down to Biloxi, Harriett had someone to talk with at the ball games. The women became close friends, and the ballplayers' wives became their own support group.

Smitty and Beverly are still married and still close friends. After their four years in the Air Force they moved back to Tonkawa, Oklahoma, and both became teachers. Beverly taught elementary school thirty plus years, and Smitty taught and coached at the high school level for more than twenty years. The community is blessed to have had two true Christian teachers willing to stay in one place for so long to positively affect multiple generations of students.

Between Smitty's right-handed slider and fastball and my left-handed curveball and change-up, we were hard to beat. In fact, the Dodger fans called us the Gulf Coast version of Don Drysdale and Sandy Koufax. Isn't it amazing that the black league compared me to the man I wanted to be like when I was a young boy? At least someone thought I looked similar. Boy, do I ever wish! And Smitty and I were only two of the strong pitching staff. I was the only left-handed pitcher in the league, and at that time the teams did not know how to hit a lefty. I guess that's why they signed me.

Me and Smitty in our Negro League uniforms

The Dodgers played teams such as Grand Bay, Alabama; the Hattiesburg, Mississippi, Black Sox; Slidell, Louisiana, and the famous Mobile Bears, who produced such players as Henry Aaron, Billy Williams, Tommy Agee, and many others. Both Smitty and I pitched against Billy Williams' brother, who was known as "The Kid." He was the Bears player/coach at the time. We played in their ballpark, which had been at one time a graveyard for old vehicles. When they dragged the infield we could see tiny, sparkling objects lying on top of the dirt.

I told Smitty, "I've heard of diamonds in the rough, but diamonds in the dirt? What is that?"

When Smitty went to the mound to warm up, he motioned for me to come to him. I didn't even make it to the mound before he said, "I better not fall down in the dirt or I'll be cut up."

"What do you mean?"

"Look. Those 'diamonds' are broken glass."

"Wait a minute," I said. "I'll check this out with our coach. This is unsafe to play on."

In a very short meeting with both coaches I was simply told it wasn't a big deal. Just play ball! Well, we played, and the fans were not happy because we beat them. We got out of town fast.

We played in some real garden spots, but one thing was sure. Wherever we went the fans loved their baseball, and the game was a way for the black communities to come together for a big social event. At some of our Sunday games the fans would come directly from church in their fine church clothes, watch the game, eat fine food, listen to fine music, make bets on every aspect of the game, and just visit. (A movie made several years ago, *The Bingo Long Traveling All Stars and Motor Kings*, paints a vivid and fairly accurate picture of life in the Bush League.)

Another game that stands out in my memory took place in Grand Bay, Alabama. Since I was scheduled to pitch, I just had to ask a few questions, such as "Where is Grand Bay, Alabama?" And "What ballpark will we be playing in?" Now, those seemed to me to be perfectly logical questions, but the ballplayers who'd been around a while couldn't believe I would be asking such questions. The manager wouldn't answer me, but directed me instead to our first baseman, "Kitty Kat" Peyton (who, by the way, was our Bush League version of Josh Gibson and the white league's Babe Ruth; he could rip it!).

I asked him the same questions I had asked the manager, and Kitty Kat replied, "Grand Bay is a little spot on the road to Florida, and everyone knows where we play when we go to Grand Bay. We play the game in my relatives' backyard."

"Say what?"

Reality set in when we got to that spot on the road, turned right at the one stoplight in Grand Bay, and headed south. It wasn't long before the asphalt gave way to gravel, which in turn gave way to dirt. And the farther south we went, the more horse-drawn wagons we saw—each one filled with people. If they weren't riding, they were walking in large groups.

Finally we pulled off to the side of the road. When I got out of the car I could see people for miles in both directions—and all were making their way to this very spot.

I waited by the car until I saw my veteran teammates start moving, because I had no idea where I was or where the ballpark might be. All I could see was a row of small houses that seemed to extend forever down the crowded road.

Well, I followed Kitty Kat between two of the houses. Once we were in the backyard all we could see were people's heads, and the mass of people were in the shape of a big U. As I made my way through the crowd it became very clear to me that we were truly in the backyard of Kitty Kat's relatives, and the backyard happened to be a pasture, and the U shape was formed around the field. I stopped, and I'm sure anyone looking at me saw my dropped jaw and the look of shock on my face.

As I stood there an elderly black man came up to me and said, "What are you doing here? Are you sure you're in the right place?"

Secretly I was probably wondering the same thing, but this is what I said: "Oh, I know I'm in the right place because my first baseman said this is the right place, and I'm the starting pitcher for today's game."

Now as I watched his jaw drop, I felt compelled to ask the old man one other question, since I had taken a closer look at the field. "I notice that there is no home run fence; the weeds are just a lot taller at a certain distance, and there are cows out there. How do I know if they hit a home run off of me?"

"First of all," he said, "they will hit home runs off of you, and there won't be any doubt about it. If the ball goes into that tall grass, either the snakes or the cows will stop your players from retrieving the ball. The players will know when to stop running."

At that point I couldn't help but laugh. I looked into the old man's eyes and said, "It's a great day for baseball; God loves you and so do I. Thanks for coming to see me beat your team." And I went out to the field to warm up. I was truly in the Bush League.

When I think about that conversation now, I recall the scene in the movie *Field of Dreams*, when the ballplayers disappear into the cornfield. I could just see my outfielders disappearing into that tall grass and never coming back.

Moments later, I approached the mound and found they had dug a deep hole, dropped a car tire into the hole, and covered it up so that only the top curve of the tire could be seen. When I threw my first warm-up pitch my cleats got caught in the tire and I fell down. Boy, did that get a big roar from the crowd! I simply stood up, brushed off my pants, and took a bow to the fans, which lessened the tension that seemed to be hanging over the field. I know it helped me relax a bit.

Before the game officially began I looked behind their backstop and saw a platform, built tree-house style, where two people were actually sitting, broadcasting the game to someone. They were also in charge of the national anthem. Every game brought with it the challenge of getting through that patriotic piece. The records were so old that the needle kept skipping, and the sound guy couldn't ever get the needle back at quite the right place, so the song jumped around a bit. It might not have been the three tenors, but at least the national anthem was always played.

As the last notes of the "home of the brave" died away, the umpire shouted, "Play ball!" and play ball we did. I'm pleased to say that the prediction of the man I had spoken to prior to the game did not come true. The home team didn't hit one home run off me—for which my outfielders were grateful—and we won the game.

Another game that stands out in my mind was one Smitty pitched in Hattiesburg, Mississippi. This was a good field with a home run fence, but it was made of tin with razor-sharp edges.

We arrived in plenty of time to warm up, which included going through a specific routine that enabled us to be ready within five minutes of game time. Smitty was in the bullpen warming up, and he told me he was ready. But as he was putting on his jacket we heard the announcer say the game would be postponed for a few minutes for a special event at home plate. We expected some sort of short recognition of a hometown player or fan, and then we would be on our way to the field. We hadn't anticipated a wedding! The game started about forty-five minutes later, and the experience was definitely a first and last for me. But again it showed just how special Negro League baseball was to the African American community, and I felt it also. Smitty had to start all over getting ready, but he survived, and I think we won that one too.

That sharp fence did become a factor, however. One of the Hattiesburg players hit a ball so hard off Smitty our center fielder took off on a dead sprint to the wall and never stopped. He ran right through the wall, caught the ball, and came out with a bloody hand from the edge of that fence—but what a catch!

Smitty's wife will never forget the day the two of them were introduced to the crowd as they entered the ballpark.

In her words, "It was too muddy to walk around the field when we arrived for a home game, so we decided to walk across the field to Smitty's bench.

"As we stepped onto the field, the announcer said over the loud speaker, 'Now entering the field is Smitty and Mrs. Smitty.'

"I was so embarrassed, but that's the way they were. I laughed then, and still have fond memories of that moment."

One of the non-game highlights for Smitty and me was visiting the Streamline Barber Shop on the east side of Biloxi and talking with the owner, Rosell Horne. In a way he was our Christian father figure in the black league. We would sit there for hours and just listen to the stories of Dodger baseball dating back to the early 1900s.

We felt very privileged to have been chosen to be a part of that rich history. We loved playing with men such as Shelby Barnes, Gary Dronet, and Johnny Thompson. We also played with a young teenager named Nate "Junior" Puryear, who went on to play Major League baseball for the Cleveland Indians and the Milwaukee Brewers. And of course playing

Smitty, Rosell, me, and our announcer, Red

with one of the sweetest hitters we ever had the privilege to play with in Kitty Kat Peyton. I will forever be grateful to Mr. Horne the barber, who was willing to break the color barrier and allow us to play for his team. He saw talent and he didn't worry about color. Coach Windham and his assistant coach, David Williams, were great coaches to play for. A part of me will always be at Main Street and Lee Street, in Biloxi, Mississippi, and the players and fans will always have a special place in my heart. I know Christ was smiling!

Smitty was fortunate to get to stay in Biloxi for his entire time in the military before he moved back home to Oklahoma, but God had other plans for me that I didn't understand at the time.

The military, in its infinite wisdom, decided it needed technical instructors at basic training where I had left just eighteen months before. They wanted me to go back to San Antonio, Texas, and teach new recruits. Of course I didn't want to go, but that doesn't matter to the military. Either you volunteer, or it volunteers your services for you. So Harriett and I, and all our possessions, were soon on our way back to San Antonio. All I could do on our way to San Antonio was to keep asking Christ, "Why me?" What could I possibly do in this new place?

After I arrived, however, I found that San Antonio boasted two semi-pro leagues—the Spanish American League and the South Texas Negro Bush League. I received approval from the base commander again to be able to play professional baseball as long as it didn't interfere with my Air Force job, which was still athletics, so it was a perfect fit.

Since I had played in the Negro Leagues, I figured I'd try the Spanish American League, so I tried out for the Alamo Enterprises and made the cut.

This team also traveled to interesting places, and the only difference between this league and the Negro League was what the visiting fans called me. Instead of "Honky," or "White Trash," I was now the only "Gringo" on my team. My team as a whole respected me and protected me while I was on the team, but I didn't have the family feeling I had with the Biloxi Dodgers. As long as I was winning everything was OK, but I was unsure how they would accept me if I lost. Fortunately for me and the rest of the team, we won our first fifteen games.

Something happened to me in the fifteenth game, however, that made me quit baseball for the first time in my life. I just walked off the field before the game and gave the coach my shirt and hat with a promise to send him the pants in the mail, which I did the next week.

What would cause me to do something like that? Well, the team had received threats before the fourteenth game, stating that if we didn't lose soon we would be "cut up."

I was given the ball the night of the fifteenth game and told to warm up; I was going to pitch the game. All the time I was warming up, my mind raced with thoughts of the threats. In between pitches I scanned the area, looking around for potential attackers. That's when I noticed the head coach arguing with the assistant about whether to start me. Finally, the head coach came over and took the ball from me—with no explanation.

I was twenty-five years old, and I had never had a coach do this to me ever. It never occurred to me that he might know something I didn't. That's when I lost it. I walked off the field without looking back.

The Lord was watching over me through that coach, though, because when I got home and turned on the news, our local sportscaster at that time, Dan Cook, was talking about a knifing incident at the park I had just left. Sure enough, a truckload of irate fans showed up at the place where we usually ate and got paid, and cut up several of our players because we won that night.

It wasn't ten minutes later that I got a call from my coach explaining why he had replaced me. He asked if I was coming back. As a whole the league was great, and some great players have come out of that league. In fact, the Mahler brothers played there and both went on to Major League careers. But after that close call, I decided to call it quits. Even though I love the game, I wasn't willing to risk my life to play! I asked to get out of my contract commitment, and the coach agreed to release me.

If I wanted to play baseball again, my only other option was the South Texas Negro League. But I didn't get serious until a black Air Force supply sergeant who worked right behind my office came over and talked to me about the league. He was a diehard fan of the league and particularly one of the teams in the league, the San Antonio Black Sox. He had heard from one of his supply buddies that I had played in the Spanish American League and had also heard why I left the league, so he asked me if he could contact the team's owner to see if he would go for a tryout, and also asked if I had a problem playing in an all-black league. He was shocked but very excited when I told him no.

A few days later he approached me again to tell me that the Black Sox owner, Mr. Royal Brock, was interested when he found out I was a left-handed pitcher. Their league didn't have too many lefties either. I found out later that Mr. Brock had called Mr. Horne in Biloxi to check me out before he took the chance, because the Black Sox had never had a white pitcher since the league was formed in 1945. In fact, when the league folded in 1979, I still held the distinction of being the league's only white pitcher. I wasn't worried about getting into any record books, though; I just wanted to play the game I loved.

On the day of my tryout, it seemed as though I drove through miles and miles of farmland down East Houston Street to the corner of Foster Road. Then, in the middle of nowhere, at that intersection, I saw a large, somewhat rundown baseball complex.

As I got closer to the ballpark, I noticed that there were a good number of cars there. I had thought I was just trying out for the owner, and it would be more private. Well, I was wrong. As soon as I parked and got out of the car, I saw a team on the field practicing, and then as I got closer to the stands I noticed a lot of people sitting there talking, drinking beer, and having a good time just watching practice.

I never will forget my first glimpse of the sharp-looking middle-aged man who approached me and introduced himself as Coach Royal Brock. His face is etched in my memory forever, because he had a smile that really helped me relax.

"I called your owner in Biloxi, Mississippi," he said, "and we had a long talk about you, so I'm very excited to see what you've got."

Then I made a really stupid comment: "Where's the owner?"

"Well, I guess you could call me the owner, but I love the name Coach much better."

After my face turned several colors of red, I put my other foot in my mouth: "Coach Brock, why are all these players and spectators here?"

"Well, Lefty—you don't mind if I call you that, do you? We all have playing names, and that sounds appropriate for you, doesn't it?"

"Sounds fine to me, Coach; whatever you think is best." I hoped my response was pulling me out of the hole I had dug for myself.

"I'm going pretty far out on a limb by bringing you on the team, and those fans up in the stands are there because they're betting on whether or not you stay. And the players are here to make sure you're good enough to make the team. You have to get some of them out, because they also know that you might just be their teammate after today."

I hadn't thought this tryout was that big a deal, but I now knew it definitely was for them. "What do I have to do to make the team, Coach?"

"I'm going to put my first four batters up, and the rest of the team will be in the field backing you up. They've been told to do the best job they can to help you get the batters out."

I then said another very stupid thing: "Coach, is this the way you try out all of your players?"

"No, but I've seen my potential players perform for other teams. In your case, I've never seen you play in person, and I have a lot riding on this because some folks don't want you out here—for obvious reasons. As far as I'm concerned, if you can play and get my batters out, you're on the team. I really don't care what color you are."

What a profound statement. Christ was smiling again! He was showing me how I was going to fulfill His plans for me. Right then I knew I had a coach/owner who was willing to give me a chance because he had an idea that I might have the skills he was looking for. The Lord had sent me my second father figure in the black league. At that moment, I felt the confidence to go out and give it my best shot. This opportunity was as exciting as trying out for college sports or for the scouts of Major League baseball. I also felt humbled that a black team would give me a chance to play in an established black league.

I stepped onto the mound and looked up into those stands. I knew most of those folks did not feel optimistic; and when the first batter came up to the plate, I was sure he was determined to do anything he could to get a hit. I stepped back off the mound, turned around toward center field, and bowed my head. My prayer went something like this: "Lord, You know I love this game and I know You have Your hand in my being right here at this moment. I also know that You have a purpose in my playing in this league that's more important than the game itself, so let's get these guys out, and go meet my new potential brothers in Christ. Amen."

When I turned around and faced down the first batter, a calm came over me that I can't explain, but I was so relaxed. The first batter grounded out to second. The next batter came up and flied out to center. The next batter and the one on deck got my attention, because both of them were just itching to knock one out of the park on me. I threw every off-speed pitch I had to both of them and struck them both out. At that moment I felt I had won the seventh game of the World Series. The whole team came in and surrounded me before I could get off the field. Every one of them, including the coaching staff, shook my hand and welcomed me to the team.

As Coach Brock shook my hand, he said something I'll never forget: "When I talked to the owner in Mississippi, I asked him more about you as a man than as a player. I knew that in this league you would have to be a certain type of person to put up with some of the things that might happen to you, especially on the road. I knew you were what we wanted when Mr. Horne said that you're a good player but an even better person. He said, 'O'Neal treats everyone the same, and he was a joy to have around our players.' I knew then that I had the right man at the right time."

His words brought tears to my eyes, and all I could say to Coach was "I won't let you down. God bless you!" As I left the park, even a few fans came up to me and shook my hand. Boy, prayer is powerful!

I was about to embark on a journey through the Bush League, Texas style, on a team that had produced several Major League players, including Cliff Johnson and Cito Gaston. Cito went on to not only play, but to become the first black manager in the Major Leagues to take his team (the Toronto Blue Jays) to the World Series and win it. He and Cliff Johnson have also been inducted into the San Antonio Sports Hall of Fame.

The first thing I had to realize was, like the Spanish American League, this league took its baseball very seriously. They were very proud of their brand of baseball, and I was going to be in the middle of that, as a white Irish pitcher. Boy, did I ever try to fit in as quickly as I could.

I had great teammates. My catcher was Concho Coleman, who could throw anyone out. He, along with my catchers in Biloxi, Shelby Barnes and Johnny Thompson, were the best catchers I ever had the privilege to throw to in my entire career. Our general manager/player, Arthur Anderson, was like my father when I was down at times. What a great human being! One of my closest Christian brothers on the team was Jim Pinchback, my right fielder. I know these three men were put into my life by Him to ensure I made it through the league. Along with Royal Brock, all of these men where men of God, and all of them are now on His heavenly team for eternity, and I know I will see them all again.

I experienced some great moments in those short two years, but three games stand out and provide a glimpse of how I existed in the Texas Negro Leagues.

The first was the first game I pitched in. I'm not sure who we were playing, but I remember the way my wife was treated when she came out to watch. You see, she hadn't felt at all uncomfortable when I played for the Dodgers, because there were other white wives she could sit with. But when we came to San Antonio, it was a different story. She went to one Spanish American League game and lasted three innings. Finally she had had enough verbal abuse and stares, so she went home and never came back. When I left that league for the black league, I talked her into attending my first pitching appearance at Black Sox Stadium. I told her it would be different; it would be like old times in Biloxi. However, I was very wrong.

Once we were within a hundred yards of the stadium, we were met by a very large sheriff with a gun on his hip. When he recognized who I was, he escorted us to my parking spot. There our car was surrounded, and the sheriff escorted my wife to her seat and me to the field. Initially I thought we were just getting VIP treatment, and I mentioned that to Harriett. Little did I know that he was there to protect her. I won the game and came running off the field to hug my wife. When I got close to her, the sheriff whisked her away to our car. After I got in the car and said good-bye to the sheriff, I looked over at Harriett. Tears streamed down her face. When she caught her breath, she told me all about the verbal abuse she had heard directed toward me, and if it wasn't for the sheriff it would have even been worse. She said he was really a nice man, and he kept telling her, "Most of that stuff people are calling Lefty is from the visiting fans. This is a new day in Black Sox history with a white pitcher on the mound for the Black Sox." He kept telling her it would get better, and he apologized repeatedly for the behavior of the fans. She really respected my teammates and home fans, and I think if it wasn't for her having to study so much on the weekends she would have come back, because she is also a woman who believes in the person regardless of their color. I wanted her there, of course, but I understood. What I love about Harriett, though, is that she didn't stop me from going. She knew I loved the game so much and that the players accepted me. She knew they would take care of me, especially on the road. They were embarrassed, and the next game I think they let the fans know about it. But even though the fans came around, I just couldn't get her back because of her commitment to graduate school.

The second game that stands out in my memory was also a home game, and I'm actually glad Harriett wasn't there for that one.

I was scheduled to start against one of the Black Sox arch rivals, the Houston Red Sox. At the ballpark I was met by a crowd of fans wishing me well, but differently, more intensely, than they had the last time. My teammates, too, kept coming up to me, encouraging me to "beat 'em bad." This game was very important to the fans and the players other than just winning, for some reason unknown to me.

While I was taking my warm-up pitches in the bullpen, a young woman came out of the stands, walked up to me, and whispered in my ear, "If you lose this game I'm going to beat your butt, but if you win the game I'll take care of you." Then she ran back into the stands.

I turned around and looked at the bench, and most of the players were laughing their heads off.

"What was that about?"

One of the guys said, "That's Shorty. She's our super fan, and she takes these games very seriously. She gets really mad when we lose, because she loses money in the stands. But if we win, she wins and shares it with us. She also works at the honky-tonk, Chilly Willie's Mustang Lounge. That's important to know if you want to get fed and paid after the game."

That was just enough information to add pressure. In the second inning I asked my catcher, Concho, to come out to the mound because I was feeling a little stressed out. I had noticed fans right behind the plate drinking long-neck beers and moving them back and forth, with money under each bottle. Every time I would pitch, those bottles would move. But when I got someone out, they would move even more, and some of the money would start disappearing. With all that going on in the stands in front of me, I was having a hard time focusing on the game.

Concho made his way out to the mound. "What's the problem, Lefty?"

When I told him, he said, "Don't worry about that stuff. That's part of the game. If they're working that hard behind the plate, then they like what you're doing. They're betting on different areas of your game. That's a good thing, Lefty, so start looking at me. Let's get this game over. I'm getting hungry." Then he gave me that little sheepish grin of his and went back to the plate. He always knew how to calm me down. We went on to win that game 6-2, and I got two hits of my own, which is rare in itself. I struck out the final batter, always a high point for a pitcher.

As I stepped off the field Shorty dove into my arms, and we both went down with a thud. She had just won a large amount of money, and she wanted me to know how much she appreciated my effort. Thank God the team came to my rescue. I knew that night would be a good one for my stomach and my wallet, and it was.

That was a big game, and we had a great post-game celebration at the lounge. I was now a full-fledged member of the team. Fans asked for my autograph or my picture with families and their kids. Coach Brock reminded me to wear my uniform so they would let me in. I'm not sure in the early seventies that too many white folks hung out there. But I was escorted into the place, and they even had a seat for me at the bar. When I looked up to get the attention of the bartender, I saw Shorty herself, grinning from ear to ear. Needless to say I didn't go hungry that night. I realized for the first time how much money was being bet on our games. The longer I sat there, the more fans came up to me to congratulate me on the win—and every one of them gave me some of their winnings. What's important here is that this tradition was maintained out of respect for the ballplayers who had given the fans their money's worth watching a game that they really loved. After that first invitation to the Mustang Lounge, I joined the team after every home game to officially celebrate there with some of the fans and players. The more I was willing to show up after the games, the closer I became to the players and the fans. It was truly a family affair, and the money was a great boost to my meager Air Force salary.

One unique and regular occurrence that I will always remember about our home games was the line of trucks backed up to the fences down both baselines whenever I was scheduled to pitch. In the back of those trucks sat white folks with their umbrellas and drinks, waiting to see me pitch. I never saw them inside the park, but they were always there when I pitched. When I got on the mound I always tipped my hat to all of them for coming out to see the game. They were also there because they knew that Black Sox Stadium was where you could see top-notch baseball!

The final memorable event of my experience in the San Antonio Bush League was our game in Mexico.

When I heard we were scheduled to play there, the first thing I thought about was how much these two races didn't get along. Add to that, a white starting pitcher. It was a disaster waiting to happen, but at that time I didn't even think twice before I agreed to pitch. Looking back, I ask myself why I had to love baseball so much that I was willing to risk everything, every time I went out to play. But baseball was in my blood, and I knew I was still capable of playing well, so I just didn't want to quit. My ego and the voice that kept saying "You can still do it" were eating at me.

The team arranged to pick me up on Highway 90 at the Southwest Military Drive overpass. Since they had several cars full of players, coaches, and fans, they didn't want to go down Military Drive, so I agreed to meet them at the overpass.

When Harriett dropped me off and saw me get into one of the cars and then disappear, all she could do was pray that I would be safe and come home unharmed. She couldn't believe I had agreed to make this trip and tried to talk me out of it, but I told her, as I always did, that the Lord would protect me. I really believed that He had a plan for me, and these experiences were all part of that plan.

When we arrived at the ballpark in Mexico, the people seemed congenial enough, even though I didn't understand a thing they were saying. Some of my teammates knew enough Spanish, so they helped me communicate, because, again, the kids wanted autographs or they just wanted to come up to me and stare and touch my skin. Every once in awhile an adult would ask me to sign a glove or a ball.

Little did I know that the only liquids in the stands were tequila and coke, and as the game progressed, I noticed a definite change in the mood of the fans, especially when I was pitching a one-hitter going into the third inning. Some of the fans started climbing the backstop just to try to rattle me.

In the top of the fifth inning I was leading 3-0, and I finally walked one of the batters. Once I got him on, I picked him off on first base. He took off for second base, and when he arrived the ball was waiting on him. The Mexican umpire called him out, and the Mexican third-base coach started arguing with the umpire. Before I knew it, the umpire had changed his call. It took only a split second for all hell to break loose. One of our infielders punched out the umpire, and both benches plus the stands emptied onto the field.

I ripped off my glove and high-tailed it for the owner's car. I got in the back, crouched on the floor, rolled up the windows, and locked the doors. Boy, did I get up close and personal with the Lord! I promised all kind of things if He would just get me out of this situation.

After several minutes, I realized it had become very quiet outside. Then I heard a rap on the window and Coach Brock's voice: "Come out. We've got a game to finish."

"You have got to be kidding! I want to go home."

"Lefty, we have a contract to finish this game, and that's what we're going to do. Don't worry; we'll take care of you. Now get back out there and win the game. Then we'll go home."

Coach had a way of making me feel comfortable in what I was doing, and I always trusted that whatever he promised me would come true.

I finished the game and we won 5-2. I was so glad when that game was over!

We had to be escorted out of the country by the Mexican authorities. After we crossed the border, we pulled in at the first rest stop we could find to unwind and reflect on what we had just gone through. We all felt very fortunate to be back on safe ground. It could have been a lot worse. Of course, I knew why we were all safe. God had heard my prayers and answered them. At that moment I breathed another prayer—this one in gratitude for His protection. I will never forget that game as long as I live. We were the talk of the east side of San Antonio, and the next time I showed up for a home game my name became permanently etched in the minds of some of the fans. Some of those fans still remember me, and at our annual old-timers games they even come up to me and say, "Do you remember that game . . . ?" I became one of the players the fans came out to watch, so life was good in the Bush League.

At the end of the summer of 1975, I was approaching the last six months of my four-year military commitment, and I was getting psyched up to go home to Arkansas and coach, just like Smitty did after his four years. We also planned for Harriett to work in the schools, just like Beverly had done. We would have identical vacations so we could get together, just like old times.

Once again, however, the military had different plans. One day a Reserve Officer Training Corps (ROTC) officer approached me and asked if I would like to become an officer in the Air Force.

"Don't they remember that I asked to be an officer the first time around, and they said no?"

Apparently that didn't matter, and soon I entered ROTC. The Lord was definitely letting me know that the Bush League phase of my life was over—for the moment.

# PART 3

# AFTER THE GAME

# Chapter 7

# LIFE AFTER BASEBALL— OR SO I THOUGHT

—⚜️◎

*Let me experience Your faithful love in the morning, for I trust You.*
*Reveal to me the way I should go, because I long for You . . . . Teach*
*me to do Your will, for You are my God. May Your gracious Spirit*
*lead me on level ground.*

—Psalm 143:8, 10

I WAS ENJOYING breakfast at the Officer Training School (OTS) in San Antonio at the cafeteria when a Captain Barnett asked if he could join me. He had learned that I was in charge of the physical training (PT) portion of OTS, and he had been given that same duty at the ROTC summer camp at our location. He wanted to ask me some questions about the OTS athletic training program.

After we talked awhile, he asked if I had a degree.

"Yes, I do."

"Would you be interested in getting a commission in the Air Force?"

I told him that I had requested becoming an officer when I first came in 1972 and had been turned down.

He said that the Air Force had a new program that allowed enlisted personnel who had a degree or at least enough hours to be able to finish the degree in two years to be able to go into the two-year ROTC program. He promised that if I took advantage of the program I would be able to get my commission and a master's degree—and the Air Force would pay for it.

This sounded too good to be true, so I added a request that I was sure would prevent my being involved in the program: "If I did this, I would want to go to only one university."

"Which one?"

"The University of Arkansas in Fayetteville, Arkansas."

What I heard next convinced me yet again that He was involved in my life. He had sent another positive Christian brother into my life. Captain Barnett said, "That's where I'm from. I'm sure I can get you a slot, but you'll have to be able to start in August."

It was now July and I had to run this by Harriett. She was so excited about getting out of the Air Force and going home, I could just imagine what she was going to say.

To my amazement, she said she would do whatever I thought was best, meaning whatever the Lord had in mind. And we knew this opportunity had to be God-directed, because it sure wasn't what we were planning.

The next thing I knew we were on our way to Fayetteville, Arkansas. Here I was becoming a student again, not a teacher, or so I thought. To show you how good God is, when I arrived at the university, I was able to get a graduate assistantship in the speech department, so I was able to teach undergraduates the basic speech class and get paid for it. Not bad, knowing my speech background. I also received a stipend from ROTC, and Harriett was able to help out and work part-time for the university.

Then, because of my undergraduate experience in college football, the coaches remembered me. I was asked to work with the special teams as a volunteer kicking coach. I worked with Coach Broyles in his last year as head coach, and Coach Lou Holtz in his first year as head coach.

Since I was in the Fellowship of Christian Athletes in undergraduate school, I searched for a chance to help out in the University of Arkansas FCA program. Coach Broyles was a tremendous Christian and one of my role models when I was growing up in Arkansas, so I was excited about the chance to work in that area.

Visiting Coach Broyles in his office as the Athletic Director

Then the Lord put in my path my next key Christian worker after His heart: Pastor H. D. McCarty, the Razorback chaplain. I became his assistant for the next two years, and we still keep in touch.

While I was on staff, I became friends with one of the football assistants at the university, but more about him later.

I also became friends with two of the young Razorback football players: Roland Sales, who had not been able to play much because he always had to be back-up to Ben Cowens and Houston Nutt, freshman quarterback from Little Rock, who had to back-up Ron Calcagni. Both kids were strong Christians and were waiting for their time to prove themselves. Through prayer and belief in themselves, both were able to fulfill their dreams. Roland replaced Ben Cowens in the Orange Bowl and broke the Orange Bowl rushing record. Houston Nutt transferred and played as a starter with Oklahoma State for Coach Jimmie Johnson. Currently Houston is one of the most sought-after head coaches for college football in the United States. Boy, does God work in mysterious but wonderful ways in our lives.

Another instance of God's wonderful work in my life came when we were at an FCA huddle one evening at the beginning of the fall season, and we went around the room and introduced ourselves.

When I said my name, a young freshman stood up and said, "Are you the same Dick O'Neal who came out to an elementary school in Conway, Arkansas, every Saturday with your college FCA athletes and played and talked with the kids of that neighborhood?"

Intrigued, I replied, "Yes, I am. This was in 1969, wasn't it?"

"Yes. And your FCA also bought those kids some basketball uniforms and had the kids play a short game at a college halftime home game."

"Yes, we did."

"Well, I was one of those sixth graders, and I will never forget what you men did, and that is a big reason why I'm here tonight."

"What's your name?"

"Marvin Delph."

Marvin became known as one of the famous "Three Musketeers" of Razorback basketball history under Eddie Sutton. (The other two were Sidney Moncrief and Ron Brewer.) Marvin went on after college and played for Athletes in Action for his Lord! This was always God's plan. We just didn't know it at the time.

Once I received my commission and master's degree, I realized my playing days in baseball were over, but if He kept putting opportunities in front of me like He had so far, then I was very willing to do whatever He had in store for me.

My first assignment as an officer was at Carswell Air Force Base in Fort Worth, Texas, and the most exciting part of that assignment was the birth of our first child, Amy Christine O'Neal. My priorities quickly changed, and Amy and Harriett were now at the top. The second most enjoyable part of my assignment was to do what I had trained to do in graduate school, making movies for the Air Force.

We stayed at Carswell for three years, but I really missed the competitive rush I got from sports, so I volunteered to be a marshal for the Colonial Invitational Professional Golf Tournament in Fort Worth, and I did that for all three years of our assignment. It was great to witness all of the pro golf athletes performing at the top of their profession. At one tournament I took a picture of a young kid who had that "golden boy" look about him. I had heard that I should keep my eye on this guy because he appeared to have some promise as a golfer. That was in 1979 and the golfer's name was Bill Rogers.

When it was time to move I requested an instructor slot in the ROTC. My higher-ranking peers felt this was a bad move and told me it would probably be the kiss of death to my career advancement, but I wanted to teach and ROTC had positions to fill. I had a long talk with my Lord, and in the end, I had His assurance that He would continue to bring people into my life who would make this a rewarding assignment.

Since we could put our top three university choices in the hat, I thought maybe, just maybe, the Air Force would select one of those schools for me. Of course I put the University of Arkansas in the mix, but since I hadn't had a chance to really be closer to my brother and his family, I also listed the University of Oklahoma as a long shot. Gary lived and still does live in Norman, Oklahoma. To be flat honest, I can't recall my third choice, but He intervened again, and we were off to Norman.

It was a great three years with Gary, his wife, Janell, and their two kids, Steve and Allen. But also, to my surprise, Barry Switzer, head coach for the Oklahoma Sooners, had hired—the same month I arrived on campus—a coach from Notre Dame as his new assistant head coach. His name was Mervin Johnson—the same Mervin Johnson who had been on the Razorback staff when I was in graduate school.

When we met it was like old times, and after a short "how are you doing" conversation Mervin asked if I wanted to work with the special team for the Sooners like I did in graduate school, if Coach Switzer would agree.

"Of course," I said, without even thinking I might have to get permission from the Air Force first.

After our meeting with Coach Switzer, I walked out of the room realizing again how powerful God is and what He can do. It didn't take long for the Air Force to agree, so there I was teaching freshman cadets in the ROTC unit, and coaching as a volunteer for the Oklahoma Sooners for the next three years.

Coach Johnson also saw how much I loved FCA and introduced me to the head of FCA for the Sooners. His name was Coach Don Jimerson, at the time the women's athletic director. From then on I helped out where I could with FCA and the downtown adult chapter, where other strong Christians stepped into my life, keeping my faith grounded. Chuck Bowman and Gary Lower still stick out in my mind. Gary is still involved with FCA as the Oklahoma state director. They were truly warriors for Christ.

I worked with Mike Keeling, the kicker and punter for the team when I arrived, and my job was to find challengers for the three special-team kicking positions. Mike was a great kicker, but he was on his way out and we had to find a replacement.

I worked with a walk-on named Tim Lasher in 1983 who really impressed me in the spring game, and I put his name in the hat as the kicker replacement. He became a skilled kicker, and his little brother, R. D., followed in his footsteps, so we were set with kickers for the next several years. Tim was also a strong Christian and has stayed involved with FCA throughout his life. I'm just proud to have been a small part of his life.

I'm congratulating Tim just after he kicked a field goal in the
Red-White Spring game.

As I reflect now on those years, I find it interesting that none of my athletic experiences at that time involved baseball. It underscored what God had said to me through my dad way back in the parking lot at my tryout with the St. Louis Cardinals: "Christ is going to work through you as a Christian player and coach to lead young men and women through the game of life His way."

After three short years in Norman, it was time to make another career decision. I liked teaching so much I really wanted to continue in that career path. While I was lecturing one day, an Air Force general slipped into the back of my classroom and observed. After class he came up and asked if I would consider moving to Montgomery, Alabama, to teach at the Air Force Air University. Once again, God had made plans; my only responsibility was to say yes and go where He sent me. I really didn't care anymore if I had anything to say about my career plans. He was doing a much better job than I, so I didn't even question the general's invitation. I accepted immediately and we were off to Alabama. I ended up teaching other Air Force personnel how to teach at the Air Force Academic Instructor School, and it was a great assignment.

Harriett worked as a speech therapist for one year until we had our second child, Richard Adam O'Neal. Once Adam came along, Harriett became a full-time mom again. To us our family was complete with a healthy daughter and son. We couldn't have been happier.

In Alabama, I didn't have an avenue to play baseball, but once I found the area FCA coordinator, John Gibbons, things began to fall into place. We started an adult chapter in Prattville, where we called home. At that time the athletic director and head football coach didn't push FCA at the high school level, so we provided a monthly breakfast devotion for any interested athletes at a local restaurant, and then took the kids to school. It was very rewarding to see those kids grow as Christians when being a Christian on campus wasn't cool.

About this time I was given my first opportunity to help area kids improve their throwing skills in baseball. It was really gratifying to see kids start at a basic level and watch them improve over time. I was chosen to help coach the Prattville teenage all-stars for all three years, and I think that was when I found my calling in the coaching arena. I had told Harriett that when I retire I want to work with kids at all levels in the baseball world to improve their skills, but at the same time teach them about the most important thing on this earth: their relationship with Him.

Through my FCA testimonial speeches around the area, I met Mike Kolen, linebacker for the undefeated 1970s Miami Dolphins and a true Christian brother. I also met a young football coach at Troy State, Chan Gailey, who has made quite a name for himself as a professional and college coach and is still coaching today. Chan and Mike, along with John Gibbons, were definitely warriors for Christ and I looked up to them all. Along with these three brothers in Christ, our church family and friends in Prattville became our brothers and sisters in Christ.

One of those young baseball players I worked with in Prattville, Kevin Turner, became a committed member of our FCA adult chapter meetings. As he grew older, he began to really love football more, and he asked me to help him learn how to punt so he could kick for Prattville. So I worked with him. He became a great running back, and I knew I had lost him as a baseball player, but he was such a great kid I kept on working with him. Our adult chapter also raised money to send him and several players to summer FCA camps, and I could really see him growing as a Christian.

Prattville made it to the state finals for the first time in their history when he was a senior. They played the big game in Birmingham where the University of Alabama played some of their games. His first punt went fifty-four yards, and as he came off the field, he looked for me in the stands. We met at the forty yard line and hugged. I was so proud of him. Prattville went on to win that game. He went on to the University of Alabama on a four-year football scholarship as a blocking back and never punted again, but that moment was special. More importantly, he was a very big part of the Alabama Crimson Tide FCA program for four years and went on to play professionally with the New England Patriots and the Philadelphia Eagles. I'm proud to have been a part of Kevin Turner's Christian growth.

Forgetting what I had learned just three years earlier—that God does a much better job handling my career than I ever could—I began planning my next move. Some of us just have to always try to fix things on our own first, and then when it doesn't work we turn to Him. I'm sure we'd save ourselves a lot of pain and heartache if we'd go to Him first!

As it turned out, all my great plans became irrelevant when I answered the phone one day.

The person on the other end said, "Captain O'Neal, this is your career monitor from Randolph Air Force Base, and I see you haven't any Headquarters experience. If you want to get promoted, you need to do your next tour here in San Antonio, at the training headquarters."

I had a hard time mustering enthusiasm for this assignment, but I knew He knew what was best, so we packed our bags and went.

This time I was going back as an officer; I knew I wouldn't have time to play baseball, so what would I do? The last time I was in San Antonio, I had played for the Spanish American League and the South Texas Negro Leagues, but that was ten or so years ago. I just couldn't see how I would be involved in sports this time around.

Contacting the local FCA office had worked before, so I tried it again when we arrived in the city. Jim Faulk, who had just left the coaching world to become a warrior for the Lord, was the brand-new FCA leader there. Since he was new and I was willing to help, we became close friends right away.

During those three years we developed a strong adult chapter in my area of town to help finance kids going to summer camps, and I continued to marshal at professional golf tournaments and help out with the golf chapel programs.

My primary job at Randolph was to do well in my new position in order to get promoted, and of course to be as good a father and husband to my family as I could. Those years went by very fast, and in the end I got promoted to major. I'd had a great life in the military, and I started thinking that if I played my cards right, I could retire at this assignment.

As soon as I started getting comfortable with this idea, I got a call from my career monitor once again, and again I couldn't believe what he said. "Major O'Neal, we have noticed that you need an overseas assignment if you expect to get promoted again. You have three choices: Kuwait, Egypt, or Turkey."

"You have got to be kidding," I said. "I was just settling in here, starting to think about retiring."

He ignored my protest and said, "So, what will it be?"

"Can I take my family?"

"Yes, you can. You'll be in a diplomatic slot in a joint command position."

That sounded important, so the news wasn't as bad as I first thought. As far as picking the country, I didn't hesitate. When I taught at Air University in Alabama I had some international students, and the best ones by far were from Turkey. My new assignment was to be the training consultant to the Turkish Air Force in Ankara, Turkey, so at least I would still be able to do what I had been trained to do.

I knew I had no choice if I wanted to get the full retirement pension, so I headed home to try to sell the family on the idea that this was a good move. That was tough. None of them wanted to go, but Harriett told the kids, "If the Air Force is willing to keep our family together for our entire career, then we'll go overseas." So, I took them all kicking and screaming to Turkey, and within six months after we arrived we found ourselves in the middle of Desert Shield, Desert Storm, and Provide Comfort, a humanitarian effort to evacuate Kurds to northern Iraq. Along with this we were there when the Berlin Wall fell and the Soviet Union crumbled. This all happened from 1989 to 1991. Just two short years!

We saw the hand of God in everything we did. He provided strong personal American and Turkish friends while we there to help us all cope with the side of the world we were in and the circumstances we faced. These folks really helped when I had to be gone on missions that I couldn't even talk about, and they still keep in touch with us.

Once, the day before I was to leave on a dangerous mission, I was praying for my family's safety and requesting peace I needed before I left. As I finished praying, our apartment guard brought me a package, which he had already checked for explosives. I opened the package and saw it was a book by Coach Barry Switzer titled *The Bootlegger's Boy*. My brother had bought the book and had Barry write a note to me before he sent it. Here's what the coach wrote: "To my old kicking coach: Keep your head low and come back to us safely. God bless you, Dick. From your old coaching buddy, Barry Switzer."

Receiving a note from one of my great coaches from the past meant so much, and for him to say "God bless you" meant even more. Again I was filled with a calm I can't explain, but I knew I could go on my mission, confident that everything would be OK.

A month later, just before I went on another mission, I received a letter from my old Razorback chaplain, H. D. McCarty, wishing me well and telling me that a lot of people were praying for my family's safety. Again I was buoyed up with the confidence that He was truly in charge.

Were those experiences just coincidences? I don't think so. He sent me Christian comforters again when I needed to be calm. Imagine having to go to work every day at a different time, return home at a different time, waiting for the guard to clear the car of bombs, always trying to sit in a different location in the car, and wearing different types of clothes when ordered to—all to avoid becoming a target for terrorists. After two years of this routine, or lack of it, I really appreciated the guards I had and the way the Turkish people took care of us.

We saw God's hand again when I flew to Istanbul to give a speech to the Turkish Air War College. When we landed, three cars and six soldiers with their drivers were waiting for me and my interpreter. We got off the plane and asked why such an escort was necessary for just the two of us.

The lead soldier said, "A terrorist group just bombed McDonald's downtown and warned that the next American who landed would be their next target."

My first thought was *Let's get out of here*, but I knew I was safer with them than without them, so we got in the middle car, and we were off to the college.

I imagined everyone we passed looked like my enemy. It was scary, but I just sensed He had a reason for me to speak to this college. We didn't stop for the light changes, and occasionally we went up on the sidewalks, scattering citizens all over the place, but we arrived at the college in plenty of time.

I got acquainted with our host officers and then went to the stage.

As I stood on that stage looking out over the audience, I was still thinking, *Why am I here?* I said a short prayer to give me strength to deliver my speech, then introduced myself in the Turkish language.

At that moment, several individuals in different places in the auditorium started applauding. After a few seconds the rest of the audience joined in, and I hadn't delivered my speech yet. My interpreter encouraged me to go on with the speech. At the end I got a standing ovation and then was told to leave the stage.

When I made my way to the area in front of the stage, a long line was already forming.

When the first officer introduced himself, he turned around and introduced several others in line. He said they were the ones who had started the applause at the beginning of the speech.

"What was that for?" I asked.

"It was out of respect that you attempted our language and that you would come even in the face of danger to talk to your past students."

"My past students? What do you mean?"

"All of these men at the head of the line were your students at Air University in Montgomery, Alabama, and they have been so excited ever since they found out you were coming. They would all like to shake your hand and invite you to their classroom to show you how they implemented what you taught them."

By the time I got halfway through the line, I couldn't help but cry tears of joy at seeing my students. The Lord had it all planned! After that time in Istanbul, I knew that nothing was going to harm me in any way as long as I trusted in my heavenly Father.

A few months before we left Turkey, He gave me and one other family member (due to limited space on the cargo plane) the opportunity of a lifetime to travel to the Holy Land. Harriett and I decided Amy was old enough to remember the trip, and someone had to stay back to take care of Adam. Additionally, since Amy and I knew some Turkish, the decision was made.

When we arrived in Israel, we walked the Stations of the Cross, retracing Jesus' steps on His way to Calvary. I stood up after kneeling where He had been crucified, and I just lost it emotionally. I cried like a baby.

Amy said, "What's wrong, Dad?"

"Amy, I'll have to tell you about my life's journey someday, and when I get to this point, I will simply tell you that these are tears of joy for what my Lord did for me personally, and how much He sacrificed for all of us."

She was only thirteen at the time, but now that she is a grown woman, I know she understood what I meant back then.

Before I knew it, the Air Force was ready for me to move again, and incredibly, they sent me back to San Antonio. There is no way I could have ever predicted that my career in the Air Force would end in the same city I started the journey, but I wasn't about to ask any questions. I was ready to make the move because I was excited about what He would do in my final chapter.

My first year back was fast and furious professionally. I became the Air Force Chief of Instructional Systems Development and oversaw the written guidance for delivering Air Force training. I had a chance to make the documents easier to read before I retired, so I set out to do just that.

The first chance I had, I contacted the FCA office to get involved with His plans for me; I knew He wanted me to continue in the sports world.

One event in this last move showed again how powerful He is. When I went to my first FCA Executive Board Meeting at San Antonio in 1992, I saw a man sitting across from me who looked familiar, but I just couldn't place him—until we all introduced ourselves.

When his turn came, he simply said, "I'm Bill Rogers."

I immediately flashed back to my time at Carswell Air Force Base in the late seventies when I marshaled for the Colonial Professional Golf Tour. I was told to take a picture of a young blond golfer on the practice green because, in the words of the fan, "That kid is going to be a special player." Just a short time later he became the PGA player of the year and the winner of the British Open. His name? Bill Rogers! Needless to say, it was the same Bill Rogers, but here I was, meeting him personally as a fellow Christian.

My son picked up the game of golf a few years later while in middle school, and the first man I called to help was Bill. So, the same man I saw as a fan in 1979 was now working with my son in 1999 as his personal golf instructor. But more importantly, Bill was teaching my son what it's like to be a *Christian* golfer.

Shortly after we returned from the Middle East, I asked Burt Hooton, a Major League pitcher from the Chicago Cubs and Los Angeles Dodgers and another of my heroes, to give his testimony at our local FCA monthly breakfast.

After breakfast he asked me, "What do you want to do when you retire?"

I didn't have to think very long before I said, "I want to work with kids on their throwing and pitching skills so they don't hurt their arms, and I want to teach in some way in the classroom."

Burt said, "He will have a place for you. Just trust Him."

In a matter of months I was asked to give coaching certification camps in baseball by another Christian friend, Frank Martin.

One day Frank asked me to come down to the office because he had an ex-Major League player in his office who wanted to get started teaching hitting in the city. But what struck me was when Frank said, "I think this guy and you will hit it off because of your strong faith and your collective walk with the Lord. Your personalities are so similar."

"Who is this guy, Frank?"

"His name is Mike Easler."

"The Hit Man?"

"Yes, they call him that."

"I'll be right down."

Mike and I talked about baseball for awhile, but the conversation quickly turned to our ride in life with Him. That set in motion a truly great Christian relationship that is still strong.

We worked together teaching kids some baseball skills as well as some Christian life skills in the process. I was also his pitching coach on a small college team that we took to the small-college World Series in Boston, Massachusetts. We made it to the finals and played the championship game at Fenway Park, home of the Boston Red Sox and Mike's former team in the majors. We lost the game, but I at least got to feel what it was like coaching in a Major League park.

When Mike became the St. Louis Cardinals' hitting coach in 1999, he invited me to spring training as his guest because he knew how badly I had wanted to play for the Cardinals in the sixties. I got to see firsthand what it must have felt like as a player and coach for a Major League club. I even got to be a part of their FCA huddle group and got to talk to some of my heroes of the sixties and hear about their walk with the Lord. Some of the past and present players I met were Lou Brock, J. D. Drew, Bob Gibson, Mark McGuire, and Jim Edmonds. I also talked with Rick Ankeil and Albert Puhols, a couple upcoming rookies. I even got to meet Stan Musial. I think if the Lord had said it

Me and Mike at Spring Training.

was time to come see Him while I was at spring training, I wouldn't have minded at all. As far as I was concerned, I had just died and gone to my baseball heaven anyway.

One last thing that Mike did on my behalf before he left the Cardinals was to wear my playing number on his uniform. He couldn't do it the first year, but after one year when I saw him on TV with my old number "19" on the back of his jersey, I broke down and cried. When I asked him about what he did, he simply said, "I wanted you to feel a part of the team as you always wanted to be. It was an honor to wear it for you."

One of those days of training kids with Mike Easler brought another key Christian brother into my life.

I got a call from the wife of a man who, I found out later, loved the game of baseball even more than I did. She had an unusual request. "My husband's birthday is coming up soon, and he really wants a pitching lesson from you, but he's too embarrassed to ask you directly."

"Why is he embarrassed to ask?"

"He doesn't think you would work with a fifty-year-old."

"Sure I would; I'm getting close to that age, too. Where is a guy playing baseball at that age?" I asked.

That was my introduction to the Men's Amateur Baseball League of San Antonio, a group of eighteen- to eighty-five-year-old men from every walk of life who loved to play the game. If it wasn't for baseball I probably wouldn't have met any of them. The game brought us all together.

After the session, my prize fifty-year-old student and president of the league, Skip Bradley, started asking me to join the league, and he didn't quit asking until I joined a few years later when I turned forty-eight.

The next four years brought me full circle in my life and love of the game of baseball. The time I spent on the bench, the field, and the road, the smells of the field and my glove, the fresh feel of the breeze, and the sweat under my hat all took me back. And thirty years seemed to have passed in a mere blink. Of course, thirty years (and more for some of those guys) had taken a toll on our bodies. We weren't physically as fast as we had been; but in our minds we still were, and that was all that counted.

Three of the men—Bill Ehrhardt, Jim Dallas, and Dick Evans—became very important to me because of their passion to learn how to teach young kids to pitch. They came to my camps when possible and always helped me in the catching chores if I needed them to. They were true believers in what I teach, and they also have become very close friends that I will cherish forever.

These men, along with my teammates on the San Antonio Rangers of the San Antonio Men's Senior Baseball League, allowed me to relive the best days of my life on the old baseball diamond and, at least for a moment, recall the innocence of the game as I remembered it at the ripe old age of five, catching butterflies in the outfield. I felt as if He were saying to me, "Dick, you deserve another chance to play your game before I see you in paradise." In response, before every pitch I would walk to the back of the mound, look up, and give thanks for the opportunity to play my game.

One game stands out in my mind when I think of what the game can bring out in an individual.

I had pitched several times and had some successes, but it was time for the Senior Texas Cup finals and we were to play a team from Houston. The game was to be played at the new professional baseball field in San Antonio, where I had already played some professional old-timers' games. It was the home of the San Antonio Missions of the Texas League.

My old pitching client, Skip Bradley, gave me the ball and told me he only needed me to go a few innings; we would bring in someone else later. It was 106 degrees and very humid, so I had no trouble agreeing to his terms. I told him I would let him know when I had had enough. After the third inning, I had to go back in the shaded area of the tunnel in the dugout, get an ice towel put on my shoulder, and drink a lot of water. I didn't think I could go another inning.

Skip came up and said, "Could you go just one more inning?"

"Of course," I said and went out there again.

After every inning he asked the same question, and before I knew it I had gone nine innings and we won the Texas Cup. It felt as if we had won the World Series. For the first time I was able to feel that same adrenaline rush I had felt so many years ago after every strikeout, pick-off play, or last pitch of the game with a called strike.

Team picture of our 2002 Texas Cup Champion team
Back Row (L–R) Bob Chabow, Dick Evans, Duane Sipila, Skip Bradley, Phil
Bepko, Bill Ehrhardt, Dick O'Neal, Jim Dallas, Bob Bepko, and Wright Ingram
Front Row (L–R) Gil Cortez, Tom Power, Bob Janzen, Pete Vega, Gilbert Martinez,
Pete Powell, and Dennis Iker

Interestingly, I've heard men all over the United States say the same thing—how baseball has revitalized their lives and the lives of others. It is truly an ageless game.

Over the next few years the San Antonio teams became a dominant force on the national scene. We have competed with more than 14,000 men from around the world at the annual Amateur World Series, held in Phoenix, Arizona. All of us meet at one time and place to celebrate the game we love so much.

# Chapter 8

# THE BOTTOM LINE

*For everyone who exalts himself will be humbled, and the one who humbles himself will be exalted.*

—Luke 14:11

ONE OF THE great highlights of my career came in 1993 when I was chosen to be a player for the Texas League Old-Timers All-Stars who were going to play the San Antonio Old Timer Dodgers at V. J. Keefe stadium on the campus of St. Mary's University. The Los Angeles Dodgers AA team (the Missions) used the stadium as their home field. Being asked to be part of the team was an honor, but what made the experience so exciting to me was the opportunity to share it with my family. How many fathers get to play in the "field of dreams" with their kids and wife around to witness it? Most kids hear their parents' stories but never get to actually relive the experience with their parents. What a dream come true!

The day before the game, the organizers held a golf tournament so the players could get acquainted or have a chance to renew old friendships. I was one of the newcomers and probably one of the youngest, at least in my mind. I felt like a rookie, getting to meet a lot of history that day. That event in itself was a dream come true for me.

They paired me up with John "Mule" Miles, whom you can read more about in the appendix.

While playing in the golf tournament, we realized we had a lot in common. He was a black ballplayer trying to break the color barrier with the hope that he would be able to play in the white Major Leagues in the fifties, and I was breaking the other color barrier in the Bush League in the seventies. I wasn't the only one who had done that, but according to the Center for Negro League Research, I was the only white guy in the history of Negro League Baseball to play in two professional Negro leagues in two different states, and that was pretty special. But neither John nor I thought anything about the color issue. We just loved the game and were willing to play wherever anyone would accept us.

As we went along John told me he used to come out to the Black Sox games in the seventies and watch me pitch, and he even put some money on me to win. He said that the odds had been in my favor. As he put it, "If you had the guts to pitch in a black league, then you had to have what it took to win. To me that was a good bet." When we finally made that connection, we became instant friends and still are. In fact, we became teammates on the Old-Timers' All-Star team for the next five years, until the San Antonio Dodgers decided not to continue the games for fear of injury to the players. That was probably a smart move.

That night, I couldn't sleep at all, anticipating the next day. Before we left the golf course, John had told me to get ready to pitch. He was going to be my manager. I felt as if I were waiting for the very first game of my life back in Pee Wee ball.

I thought the appointed time for us to go to the ballpark would never come, but it did. Adam, who was nine years old at the time, and I went out to the ballpark at three thirty that afternoon, which was about two hours before the game. The rest of the family came later.

When we approached the players' gate, a security guard asked me to verify my name on the players' list. When I looked down and saw my name, my dream of being recognized as a professional baseball player again officially became reality. I'm sure my son didn't have a clue what I was feeling, but he would soon, very soon.

We no sooner walked through the gate, hand-in-hand and me with my Cardinal gear on, when I was mobbed for autographs. I hadn't realized that a lot of fans showed up early to buy and trade baseball cards at a card dealers' show in the ballpark. I had thought by showing up early, Adam and I could have some quiet time together so I could attempt to tell him what this event was all about.

After signing autographs for a few moments, I looked up, trying to find Adam. We had gotten separated in the crush of people at the gate. When I spotted him, he looked at me wide eyed, his mouth hanging open, as if to say, "What are those people doing to my dad?"

Once I was done, we grabbed hands again and continued our walk to the field.

Adam said, "Dad, what did they want your autograph for?"

"Because I'm one of the old-timer baseball players they came to watch. By getting our autographs, they'll have a piece of history to remember and keep for their kids."

It sounded like a good answer to me, but after a small pause, Adam said, "Get this straight; you're just my dad." His simple statement brought me back to reality quickly; I knew he was right.

Smiling, I got down on my knees, looked him straight in his shining eyes, and said, "You're right, son, and I hope I make you proud of me tonight when I play the game I love. Remember, regardless of what happens tonight, I'm proud to be your dad." I will always cherish that moment with Adam, and I know the Lord was with us. He used Adam to humble my heart and bring me back to reality.

We continued our walk to the dugout, and Adam asked if we could throw some like we did at home. I couldn't help but remember another young boy who stood on a tree root in the backyard and threw to his dad. Isn't it amazing how history repeats itself?

As we warmed up, fans kept coming by for autographs, and I took care of every one of them. I never tired of this part of the game. I have warm memories of the pros in various sports who took the time to autograph things for me when I was a child, and I also have negative memories of those who refused to sign. But all of this seemed to just get in Adam's way of enjoying playing catch with his dad.

When my golfing partner from the day before, "Mule" Miles, showed up, he asked Adam if he wanted to be the batboy for the game. Boy, that made Adam's day. Now he could sit on the bench with his dad. John will never know how much I appreciated him doing that for my son.

#8 Miles, #10 my son, and me getting ready for the 1994 Old Timers game
at the new Dodger AA Mission stadium

Other players started showing up, some of whom I had watched on
TV for years at the Major League level—Burt Hooton, Cliff Johnson,
Mike Easler, Luis Tiant, Glenn Hoffman, Jerry Grote, Bob Bruce, Odie
Davis, Jimmy Wynn, Joe Sambito, Gary Bell, Joe Horlen, Nate Oliver,
John Shelby, Ken Pape, and Sam Harshaney. Other notable players were
Rocky Thompson, Roy White, Don Falcon, and even the mayor of
San Antonio at that time, Nelson Wolff. He had played in the Spanish
American League growing up and still plays in the Men's Amateur Senior
Baseball League today. These were just a few of the great ballplayers I
met that day. There were also other players there who had dreamed of
playing in the majors but were as excited as I was just to participate in
the Old-Timers' Classic. I truly felt like I was in my "field of dreams."
I was waiting for the ballplayers to disappear into the cornfield, but
thank God they didn't, and my son didn't either. He was really getting
into the event.

When we were all introduced, I kept looking at Adam to get his
reaction. I don't think he had realized that I was going to pitch against
some of these players.

Before the game started Mule told me he wanted to save me for last. He would let the older pitchers, and of course, famous names, pitch first. After all, I was a rookie. Boy, have I heard that a lot in my life.

As Adam and I sat and watched, I tried to give him a crash course on who these guys were, and I kept reminding him to never forget this moment. I'm not sure why I felt I had to remind him, because he was asking me all kinds of questions.

Since we only played three innings, those first two just flew by. Before I knew it, Coach Miles was calling for me to warm up. At that moment I realized that even though I never made it to the majors, the good Lord was giving me a rare opportunity to pitch to a few of the ones I would have pitched to if I had made it. It was almost as if the Lord had already been planning this moment from the very beginning of my journey so that others would be able to read about it and learn that if we trust in Him we will find fulfillment.

I walked to the mound and started warming up, and I could feel my heart racing. When the announcer said my name as the new pitcher for the Texas League All-Stars, I didn't think I was going to be able to continue. I looked over at the dugout and saw my close Christian brother John Miles with his arm around my son as though they were one, encouraging me on.

All of a sudden I heard Adam say, "Come on, Dad. You can do it! Strike them out!" After a glance at the rest of the family in the stands, I was ready to go.

The umpire behind the plate, Satch Davidson, was also a special person. He had been the umpire behind the plate when Henry Aaron hit home run 715. It was an honor to have him officiating.

The first batter up was Burt Hooton, whom I had admired for years as a pitcher for the Chicago Cubs and Los Angeles Dodgers. And of course, he was the guy the Lord had brought into my life earlier who said, "He will have a place for you. Just trust Him."

He fouled a few off and I threw a few balls. It went to a full count, and I grooved one right across the plate. He hit it on a line right past my ear and into centerfield. I still don't know how I kept from getting hit. I said to myself, "That's got to be at least a double." When I turned and saw my centerfielder, Roy White, running the ball down, I felt as

Me on the mound

if I were seeing the game in slow motion. I then thought Burt would probably get a triple, but when I turned around and saw Burt running, he also appeared to be running in slow motion. He hadn't even gotten halfway down the first base path by the time Roy fielded the ball and threw it back into the infield. My dream of playing just like I used to quickly turned into the reality of aging. My mind and heart were young, but my body—and obviously everyone else's bodies—had slowed down a bit. I suddenly felt like a very old rookie. I also realized that this game was definitely for the fans to see the old players they remembered on the field again in their old uniforms. Clearly, I wasn't there to strike everyone out, but just to enjoy the game and fellowship with the players.

The next batter, Jerry Grote, the catcher from the famous 1969 Mets, grounded out, and I got booed. Again, I was reminded that the fans had come to see the players hit the ball and try to run around the bases.

Cliff Johnson approached the plate next, and I knew what the fans had come to see from Cliff: a home run, since that's what he did very well in the Major Leagues. I went to a full count with him too. The next pitch was a change up, and he swung and struck out. Again, the boos came raining down on me, but this time I just took a bow and waited for my next victim.

The next batter up grounded out, and it was time to leave the game. I didn't want to leave the mound, but my body said, "Go hug your son before you get hurt."

The most important moment happened when I crossed the white line on my way to the dugout. My son met me there and hugged me. "You were great, Dad," he said. "This has really been great and I'm proud of you." Once again, at that moment the good Lord could have taken me home to my heavenly mansion in the sky, and I would have been satisfied. I was thrilled that my family had been a part of this historical event, and I felt blessed that my kids had a chance to see what their father loved to do and got to see him live out his final dream. My journey was complete.

After the game the Dodgers hosted a cookout for us and our families while the AA Dodgers played the real game. This piece of the evening was equally priceless. Adam got to get all of the big-name autographs and had his picture taken with them. The rest of my family, too, got to hear all the stories of how other players had made their journeys in baseball.

I mentioned to John Miles that these stories should be captured somehow for historical purposes. He just looked at me and said, "Tell your story, and in doing so you will have told our stories too." His comment provided the inspiration for this book.

The book has been another journey that I thought wouldn't have taken as long as it has, but again, when I started taking too much control of the project, the Lord would step in, and I would reflect and pray about what I was doing. He would always say to me, "My son, it doesn't matter how long it takes; when it is finished the book will make a positive difference in the lives of those who read it."

I can think of several great "bottom lines" that I've learned. For example, "What goes around comes around"; "Be nice to people on the way up, for you will surely meet them on the way down"; or "Don't miss an opportunity to love your wife and children, and be there for them through both good and bad times." Jim Valvano—a great college basketball coach but an even greater person in the game of life—while fighting the cancer that ultimately took his life, said, "Don't give up; don't ever give up." To me those are great reminders in life.

But the bottom line at the very bottom, so to speak, is that everyone has a story to tell and a legacy to pass on. It doesn't matter if it's in the form of a book to inspire, a short quote to motivate, or simply living the right example for your kids to follow. Pass on your legacy so it will live well beyond your lifetime. When given the opportunity to share your life with your family, or the rest of the world, do it!

On the road with Up With People "What Color is God's Skin" became my theme song for life, but another of the group's songs, "Where the Roads Come Together," wraps up my life's journey pretty well. It talks about how everyone is different—their hearts beat uniquely; their souls are free to be different. It reminds us that the walls we build are only in our minds, and as we journey through life we find that everyone has a purpose and that someday we will all meet again "up the way."

After reading my journey, I trust it's clear where my "up the way" is!

Never assume your dream is impossible! My dad told me to live life in such a way that I wouldn't have regrets when I was older. Even though my dad has passed away I know he is proud of me, because I did what he asked; I have lived my life to its fullest and fulfilled my lifelong dream of playing baseball in a *major* way. What a journey it's been, and God was there—through every joy, every disappointment, every triumph, every loss. All glory and honor belongs to Him!

# EPILOGUE
## THE REUNIONS

*LORD, I have heard the report about You; LORD, I stand in awe of Your deeds. Revive your work in these years; make it known in these years.*

—Habakkuk 3:2

WHEN I RETURNED to the States in 1991, after the Gulf War, I went to see if the old Black Sox Stadium was still standing. I found only an empty field. I felt lost and alone because I thought I would never see the players again. However, I got busy with my life and the idea grew dimmer as years went by. Even after the Old-Timers' game in 1993, when the other players said we needed to write our history and also get together more often, I still didn't get the hint from Him. I was so wrapped up in trying to decide what I was going to do in retirement and making that transition that I didn't pay much attention to anything else.

In 2004 I was delivering a workshop in Dallas that dealt with information I had learned in the Air Force. In my opening remarks I happened to mention that I had played professional baseball in the Bush Leagues. At our first break, a student came up and asked if she could give a friend my phone number. Her friend was a historian of Negro League baseball, and she thought he might be interested in what I had to say. I said, "Sure," and went back in class.

After class I went to my hotel room and found a voice mail from Dr. Layton Revel, director of the Center for Negro League Baseball Research, asking if he could come over to the hotel that night, meet me, and have me autograph some baseballs. I was anxious to know if the guy was legitimate, so I agreed to see him.

We had a great conversation, and I felt comfortable enough to share many of my experiences in those leagues. As he left, he said he would contact me again after he checked out my stories to make sure they were accurate. That in itself made me feel more confident that he knew what he was doing.

It wasn't long before Dr. Revel got back in touch with me to let me know that he was very interested in learning more about the Texas Negro Leagues. He had interviewed several black ballplayers in the Texas leagues and found out that I was indeed the guy known in those days as Dick "Lefty" O'Neal. He told me he attended Negro League reunions all over the country, and the lightbulb went on in my head. Here was the man who could help us organize and execute Texas league reunions. My next Christian brother was now in place.

Me, Miles, and Dr. Revel at a Negro League function in Austin, Texas

We agreed to get together to see if it was possible to have a reunion in San Antonio. We found a man from my past who was still alive, and when Dr. Revel mentioned his name, I lost my breath for a moment: Arthur Anderson, one of the founders of the South Texas Negro League, and the same man who had welcomed me with open arms on the day of my tryout in 1974. We met with Arthur and his lovely wife only to find out that he was very close to dying. It was so exciting to hear Arthur again but also so sad to see his physical state. It was hard to look at him, because I remembered him as that strong, athletic-looking, handsome man who became my father figure when I was just a young airman. He was frail, yet his contagious personality still shone through. He was so happy to see me and told Dr. Revel a few things about me that were very humbling.

When we told Arthur what we were trying to do, he said we needed to contact Everett Turner. Everett was a player for the Black Sox before I came along, and he was also retired from the Air Force. Arthur thought Everett, Dr. Revel, and I working together could make the reunions happen.

When we left, Arthur gave me one of the old pitching jackets that we wore as a memento for my contribution to the team. He knew I would cherish and keep it. He also told us that we needed to move fast, because he didn't have long on this earth and he had been dreaming of this for a long time. When I heard that, I knew the Lord had been working through Arthur.

We contacted Everett Turner, told him about our meeting, and pleaded with him to help us put on a reunion. Out of that meeting came a true Christian relationship between Everett, Dr. Revel, and me that will last forever. We knew we could accomplish anything with His help.

We got right to work planning the gathering. Everett and I would locate the players, and Dr. Revel would research their histories and have plaques made from the Center for Negro League Baseball Research to present to the players at the reunion.

After just a short three weeks for us, but what I'm sure felt like an eternity for Arthur, we held our first South Texas reunion at the old honky-tonk Mustang Lounge, where we had all hung out during our playing days.

Twenty-five ballplayers and their families attended our first reunion, sixty-three people in all. Some of those people were our fans who had been with us throughout the existence of the league. In fact the first fan to hug me was Shorty, the woman who had confronted me at our home game, telling me to win or else!

The moment Dr. Revel, Everett, and I still cherish the most from that night was the entrance of Arthur Anderson and his family. He was so dressed up and carried himself with as much dignity as he could muster as he leaned on his walker. He stopped to talk to all of the players individually and shared all of it with his family that night. He signed anything anyone wanted signed and smiled from ear to ear the entire time. When he received his plaque I couldn't help but cry. I knew at that moment that part of God's purpose in these events was bringing peace to Arthur—body, soul, and mind—for just one night.

Arthur signed his name many times that night.

A few days after the reunion, Everett and I got a call from Arthur's wife. She said Arthur had made peace with his Lord and had gone to be with Him. She also told us that Arthur had been waiting for the reunion to come so he could go to be with His Father in heaven. He wanted us to know, she said, how proud he was of us for getting the event together and that he would be looking down on the reunions to come. She ended the conversation by inviting us all to his funeral.

When we arrived, the church was packed. People even stood in the back. Arthur's wife asked if I would say a few words about Arthur on behalf of the ballplayers who were there. She also wanted me to be one of the players to carry Arthur to his final resting place.

When I got up to speak, He gave me the words. I said, "Arthur Anderson was my father figure in Negro League baseball in San Antonio. When everybody around me in my life thought I shouldn't play for the Black Sox since I was white, Arthur Anderson said I should. Arthur Anderson was the one who met me at the ballpark for my tryout. He assured me that he would be there for me and told me not to let anyone or anything stand in the way of my playing the game I love. When I made the team, Arthur was as proud of me as anyone on the team. More importantly, I thank Arthur for being the Christian man that he was. The Lord knows Arthur Anderson personally! He is the reason all of his fellow ballplayers are here today. He has touched us all profoundly in one way or another."

In honor of Arthur's final words—that he would be looking down on our future reunions—we decided to have another gathering at the old honky-tonk. We found more ballplayers, and again the event was a success.

I got the shock of my life when an elderly man with a cane came through those doors and said, "Hey, Lefty! Remember me?"

It took looking into his eyes to realize that it was my old buddy who caught for me in all of my games for the Black Sox, Concho Coleman. I thought he had already passed away, and he looked so old. He was actually two years younger than I, but life hadn't been very good to him. However, he still had that spunk that had kept me laughing through all my games; he was the master of keeping me loose. We talked for a long time, and he gave me a glimpse into what he'd been doing for the last thirty years—no wonder he looked so old.

When it came time for Concho to receive his plaque that night, Dr. Revel told everyone the story I had shared with him when we had first started planning these reunions. He had asked me which of the catchers—of all of the men I had been so fortunate over my years of baseball to throw to—was the best. I said without hesitation, Concho Coleman. I was sitting next to Concho when Dr. Revel shared the story, and it was so special to see how Concho lit up the room with his smile. Then he looked at me, we shook hands, and neither of us really wanted to let go. His grandson was also there, and he was very proud of his grandpa. You could tell he was touched. That one moment made my night, and again He was showing my life flashing right before my eyes.

Why did I mention that story as the highlight of that evening? Because only a few weeks later Concho passed away! Again Everett, several ballplayers, and I went to the funeral. But this funeral was totally different from Arthur's funeral. It was held in a chapel, and there were probably only twenty-five people there—and that included family and our ballplayers.

After sitting for awhile I walked up to the open casket to say good-bye to my friend. What I saw next to his head almost made my heart stop: it was my baseball card. I had given it to him the night of the reunion and written on it, "God bless you, Concho. Your brother in Christ, Lefty O'Neal." I turned around in tears and asked his family why that card was there.

One of them said, "That was one of his wishes, that the card be with him forever."

His mother asked if I would say a few words about Concho, and the Lord faithfully provided them when I needed them. He wanted me to assure them that Concho was a very important part of Negro League baseball and to remind them that even though they didn't believe his stories of those baseball days, they were true; and they should be proud of him. After the funeral the family couldn't stop asking all kind of questions about Concho, so it was an honor to have shared what I felt about him.

The timing of these reunions was so amazing, and only He could have made them happen when they did. Of the players in Negro League baseball, I'm probably one of the youngest and the oldest is ninety-four. Most of these players were in their thirties and forties when I was playing with them in my twenties. I think these reunions are His way of recognizing on earth as many as possible before they all pass away, because, quite frankly, they never were publicly recognized when they should have been. They can now leave a public legacy to their families.

The third reunion took place in 2005 and was unique because we held it as part of one of the San Antonio Missions AA professional games. We could present the plaques, and the players could be available to the fans if they wanted autographs. The Missions staff set aside an area for us to sign autographs, thinking we'd be done in plenty of time to watch the game. Well, to their amazement and ours, we signed autographs for eight innings.

The reunion was a total success, and according to Dr. Revel, it was the largest Negro League reunion in the nation. We contacted fifty-two ballplayers and forty-eight of them showed up. Dr. Revel also presented memorial plaques to Arthur Anderson's wife, the Royal Brock family, and the Odie Davis Sr. family, because they founded the league in 1945.

Group picture at Mission Stadium

We tried to do the same thing in 2006 but were only able to get twenty-five ballplayers to attend. With each year, more were failing physically, either through illness or death.

After that reunion I started thinking of all of those players I played with in the Gulf Coast Negro Leagues, especially when Hurricane Katrina nearly wiped the Gulf Coast off the map. I wondered how many players had survived the storm and how many of them had kept in touch with each other.

I mentioned my concerns to Dr. Revel, and he said, "Why don't we do there what we've done here?"

I told him that I would start trying to find players, and the first one I located was my old coach, Coach Windham. He sounded just like I remembered, and he was so excited to hear from me.

When I told him the idea about the reunion, he said, "That would be great. It would give us all something to smile about."

I knew at that moment that, again, God was a part of this event. Coach Windham took on the task of finding ballplayers and providing their names and phone numbers to me and Dr. Revel so we could get plaques ready to present in Biloxi, Mississippi.

A few months later, I flew in to help Coach Windham with the last-minute details. Dr. Revel arrived the next day. My old white pitching buddy and lifelong friend, Smitty, and his wife drove down for the event.

On the last leg of my flight to Biloxi, a black man sat next to me, and we struck up a conversation. He asked what business I had in Biloxi, and I said that I was going to a baseball reunion.

"What kind of baseball reunion?"

"The Gulf Coast Negro League reunion."

"Oh yeah, I read about it in the paper. That sounds interesting. I ought to check it out. What's your name?"

"Dick O'Neal."

"Dick Lefty O'Neal?"

"Yes."

"Your name was in the paper. The paper did a great job advertising the event. Do you need any help?"

I mentioned that we might need more food. He gave me his card and told me to come see him the next day at his office. I looked at the card and could not believe what I saw. He was in charge of a local grocery store. Only the Lord could have orchestrated that meeting.

When we got off of the plane, my old coach was there to meet me. We hadn't seen each other since 1972, and it was now 2007. We hugged and then I introduced him to my new friend. The man was so excited to meet Coach Windham and invited him also to his office the next day.

Before Coach Windham took me to Keesler Air Force Base he took me to the east side of town to show me the aftermath of Katrina. Most of the homes I remembered were not there anymore. When he took me to the old ball field where we played our home games, I saw that the entire stadium had been turned into a FEMA mobile home park for people who had lost their homes. The only thing that reminded me of the old days was the scoreboard down the right field fence. The football stadium parking lot next to our stadium was now a Salvation Army mobile kitchen for homeless people. Our event happened sixteen months after Katrina, and this was still going on.

Then the coach surprised me and took me over to see my old first-base buddy, "Kitty Kat," because he knew how special our relationship was, and also because Kitty Kat was going to cook for the event. Coach wanted to tell him the good news about the food. When we played, Kitty Kat was always cooking something for the team so we could eat and drink together after the home games. After all of these years Kitty Kat was well known for his barbeque.

When I arrived at his house, it was like stepping back into 1972. Nothing had changed, and Kitty Kat was out back in his cooking shack, as usual, cooking.

When I came up to him, I said, "Sir, I have heard that you were once a very famous baseball player. May I have your autograph?" He seemed confused at first, but then he looked into my eyes.

"Is that you, Lefty?"

"Yes, it is," I said, and we embraced. The world stood still for just a moment. I had never thought we would see each other again, and here we were.

When I told him that food was no longer an issue and asked for a list of what he needed, he was speechless.

Once we had our list, we were off again to check into my room at Keesler Air Force Base. Just entering the gate of Keesler and checking into my room brought memories flooding back. The last time I had been there was 1972, and here I was again in 2007. I said good-bye to my coach and told him to meet me at the grocery store the next morning.

When we arrived at the office of the man I met on the airplane, we found out that he had also invited his deputy in for the meeting, since he was a baseball fan. Dr. Revel had arrived and was also invited to the meeting. When introductions were over, the chief and deputy realized that Coach Windham was a football official and baseball umpire all of those years, and they didn't even know about his days with the Biloxi Dodgers. This was another meeting that I had nothing to do with. Dr. Revel and I just sat back and enjoyed the conversations.

My friend from the plane gave me some coupons and said, "Just go get what you need."

As we left, Coach Windham asked if they would be at the reunion. They said absolutely, and we went on to collect our needed supplies.

We all took the food to Kitty Kat so he could keep cooking. I also wanted Dr. Revel to meet him, since I had talked about him so much. It was so much fun watching Kitty Kat share with Dr. Revel those days in the Gulf Coast League.

With assurances to Kitty Kat that we'd be at the reunion site in time to set up, we left to meet Smitty and Beverly at the base.

After more introductions, I sat back and listened to Dr. Revel and Smitty talk about our days in the league. I really enjoyed hearing other players' perspectives on that time in our lives.

The next day we all followed Coach Windham to the new baseball facility at Biloxi High School, which we had never seen before. It turns out that both the coach of the high school team and the athletic director of the school had played in the Gulf Coast League a few years after I had left. They were definitely excited and had planned the reunion around a double header.

The recognition of the Negro League players took place between the two high school games so the high school kids were able to see history right in front of their eyes and also see their coach and athletic director be a part of that history. We had plenty of food, and our friends from Keesler were there also to be a part of the event. It was so gratifying to step back and watch players embrace each other not only because of baseball but because I'm sure they were relieved to know they all had

Group picture in Biloxi

made it through Katrina. When the plaques were presented, the players' faces shone with joy at being remembered for who they were and what they had done during those days.

One final encounter topped off the day. We took the leftovers back to Kitty Kat's house and had another get together. Some of the players who couldn't be at the earlier event came over for the evening affair. I noticed a couple of black men who had looked at me several times during the day but had never come over to say hi. I had asked Coach Windham who they were, and he said they were some of our most devoted fans and would probably be at the evening event.

Coach was right, and after some food and drinks the two men approached me. One of them said, "Lefty, do you know who I am?"

"No, I don't believe I do."

"You used to give me a nickel for every ball I retrieved. The folks at the stadium would give money sometimes but mostly candy. But you always gave me a nickel. I was known as the "nickel-a-ball boy."

"Good grief! Sure, I remember you. How are you doing?"

"I'm doing fine. I bet you don't remember this guy either."

"No, I don't, but refresh my memory."

"I was the kid you gave a quarter a game to count pitches, so you would know when to change pitchers."

"Oh yeah!"

"Nickel-a-ball boy" then said, "Since you and Smitty were the first white men we had seen pitch in the Negro Leagues, we would come up to you and rub your skin to see if it would turn black."

"Oh yes, I remember now, and I also remember you two were always together. How old were you guys when you did that for me?"

"We were nine and ten."

"Isn't it amazing that you're still together after all these years?" I said. "How old are you now?"

"Forty-four and forty-five."

Boy, did I feel old! The word *reunion* took on a whole new meaning for me. "What are you two doing now?"

They said that because of their time together at the ballpark and my treating them with respect and just having fun with them, they decided that they would live in the same town and maybe go into business together. One of them continued, "The money we made doing things for you was special because you didn't care about our color. You just saw two boys who needed help and wanted to be a part of the team, and you saw to it that we were. Since we grew up, you have been sort of our Christian model for us and our kids. We will never forget your kindness toward us, and we've tried to live the way you taught us. God bless you, Lefty, for what you did then and what you and Dr. Revel have done for all of us today."

It was so hard to hold back the tears, not just because of what they said, but because it was also Him telling me, through these people, that my journey was worth it.

These reunions have taught me several things. One lesson I learned is that we never know what simple acts of kindness will do for a person's self-image and how it will affect his future. I also was reminded by Him just how small this world is, and we never know how many people we will have the opportunity to touch. And finally, as my earthly father told me in that parking lot when I was a seventeen-year-old-boy, "Go out and be a fisher of men and women for Christ and you will be rewarded." Well, I have definitely been rewarded already, and my life is not over yet. I just want to leave the earth better off than the way I found it, one person at a time.

I've coached a lot of kids on how to improve their throwing and pitching skills, but before they went off to college and professional baseball I always tried to remind them to use the sport as a platform to glorify Him. I also reminded them that if they did that, they would be rewarded in the end and for all eternity. I planted the seed; it was up to them to allow Him to work it out in their lives.

I wait for the next reunion with great anticipation; and if it's not on this earth, there surely will be even a better one waiting for me when it is time to meet my heavenly Father!

If you have a story to tell, then tell it. If you love the Lord, then share Him with someone. Since you only have a short time on this earth, make it a top priority to look for the good in people. And if you haven't had a reunion of some kind, make one happen!

On behalf of Him, all of my Christian brothers and sisters, and of course the guardian angels I anxiously await meeting, may the Lord hold you in the palm of His hand forever. Amen.

# APPENDIX
## AN INTERVIEW WITH
## A LIVING LEGEND
### *"I'M NOT COMPLAINING; I'M JUST EXPLAINING"*

*If you forgive people their wrongdoing, your heavenly Father will forgive you as well. But if you don't forgive people, your Father will not forgive your wrongdoing.*

—Matthew 6:14–15

THE FOLLOWING IS an excerpt of an interview from a *local* newspaper with a staff sports writer that John "Mule" Miles and I agreed to do to help raise funds to send athletes to the Fellowship of Christian Athletes camps. When I listened to the questions regarding how he was treated playing for an all-white team, and more importantly how he handled the situations, it brought back memories, and my prayer is that his words will inspire those of you who have a passion for something, but the odds are against you.

**Interviewer:** Why did you play baseball?

**John:** I loved baseball and I was willing to play it anytime, anywhere. When I started, that became a problem sometimes because of the time it took away from the family. When I started playing for money, it wasn't enough to make a living on. You've got to understand that this was during the forties and fifties. The only baseball players making any kind of money were the ones in the majors. The minor leaguers were making little or nothing themselves. And a person of color didn't

Me and John being interviewed

even have a choice with either of those options. Our only choices were the Negro Major Leagues, which was short lived, or semi-pro bush or barnstorming leagues. So that's where my money had to come from. But let me reemphasize I was not playing for the money anyway, and at that time not many of the major leaguers were thinking of the money that much either. We just loved the game, and if someone was willing to pay to watch me, that was fine. I think that's what I don't like about the game today. Too much emphasis is placed on the money and not the game. That's why we have overinflated egos running around as ballplayers. But I must say that the ballplayers aren't at fault as much as the management who allowed it to happen.

**Interviewer:** Have you ever played on an all-white team, or played against an all-white team? If so, how were you treated?

**John:** I recall playing on an all-white team in Laredo, Texas. I was the only black. We were playing in Corpus Christi. After the game we went to eat at a restaurant. There were seventeen ballplayers and coaches in all, and when we went in, the restaurant manager said they couldn't feed the black ballplayer. He would have to leave. Well, the ballplayers and coaches got together and told the manager that if their player didn't get to eat they wouldn't either, so the manager reconsidered and I got to eat with the team. I really felt proud of what the team did, but you see, the players were looking at me as a teammate and not a black person. I think Dick "Lefty" O'Neal said the same thing about his experience when he was on an all-black team.

You see, in sports, unlike any other profession, the color barrier comes down quicker. That's another reason why I loved the game so much. It was a place where I could be treated as an equal. Oh yeah, there were times when I still knew my place. In fact, after that meal I still had to stay in a different motel because the motel manager wasn't willing to bend even if the entire team didn't stay at the motel. But even when that occurred, the coach made sure I had transportation to get back to the team from my motel for blacks. He also apologized for the inconvenience. At that time what the coach did was more than enough for me because he was sincere.

You know, I think Lefty O'Neal has already mentioned that the kids at the ballparks flocked to him, wanting to touch him to see what his white skin felt like and to see if the color would change to black when they rubbed his skin. He also said they wanted to touch his hair to see how it felt because it looked different. They also wanted his autograph and a picture with him whenever they could, while the adult fans, especially the visiting adult fans, kept their distance from him. That same thing happened to me with the white kids. And like Lefty said, "Oh, the innocence of a child! When do we lose the innocence of a child?"

When I started playing for the Negro Major Leagues for the Chicago American Giants I remember playing an all-white team at their ballpark, and, boy, did we hear the verbal abuse. I remember being in the on-deck circle warming up to hit, and one white fan hollered as loud as he could and looked right at me and said, "This must be Nigger Night." I looked back at him and said, "Yeah, and we are going to have a big one too." My coach came up and told me to ignore him and take my frustrations out on the ball and the pitcher. Let your bat do your talking. I had a great night that night, and when I would pass that fan I would just smile. I think that smile of mine every time I scored shut that guy up for good for at least that night. That night at the ballgame is when I truly learned how to take the abuse. I don't think the fans realized that the more they talked the better we became and that they were sometimes the reason their teams ended up losing. I also learned, and I think Lefty O'Neal also said it, that if you talk the talk then you better walk the walk. In other words, if you want to talk big, you better back it up with a great ballgame. The best way is just to keep your mouth shut, unless you are going to say something good, and let your actions speak for themselves. Lefty was a great white ballplayer to watch in an all-black league because, you know, he used those negative comments and names such as "white trash" and "honky" to his advantage, and the home fans loved him because he was a positive role model.

I watched him play in the seventies for the San Antonio Black Sox because we had a lot in common and that's also why we have been close Christian brothers ever since. Our fans in San Antonio came to the ballpark to be entertained, and a lot of them bet on the game also. When I saw Lefty pitch I knew why the coach signed him. He was a winner, and he knew how to take all of the pressure that was coming his way. I even put some small bets in on him because I knew he always had a chance to win. And I also could relate to what he was going through. He still says to this very day that he uses the phrase he heard from me when asked to talk about this game of baseball. He and I always start our conversations with "Just remember I'm not complaining; I'm just explaining." And it's true! We are just explaining our small part in the big game of life.

**Interviewer:** When you die, what do you want people to remember about you?

**John:** I was a good man and a good husband to my wife and a good father to my kids. To the community I want to be remembered as a decent man who loves the Lord, and a great ballplayer who wanted to give back to his community in the way of working with kids and getting them involved in sports instead of drugs and gangs. I also want them to know that it was people like Dick "Lefty" O'Neal who reminded me that maybe I might have made a difference in a young kid's life that is having problems being accepted, that maybe baseball was a game for everyone to play without regards to race, color, or religion. Maybe, just maybe, what we learn in sports we can apply to our daily lives. Lefty and I are only two of many who came before us who feel the same way.

The Lord will have a special place for John "Mule" Miles in heaven. I only hope I get to play on his team when the Lord takes us home.

I think it is only appropriate to end this appendix with the way John ends his presentations: "May the road rise up to meet you. May the sun shine softly in your face. May the wind be always at your back, and until we meet again, may the Lord hold you in the palm of His hand. Amen."

John has been inducted into the San Antonio Sports Hall of Fame, and remains one of my closest brothers in Christ. God bless you, John!

# REDEMPTION PRESS

To order additional copies of this book, please visit

www.redemption-press.com

Also available on Amazon.com and BarnesandNoble.com

Or by calling toll free (844) 273-3336

CPSIA information can be obtained at www.ICGtesting.com
Printed in the USA
LVOW08s2334050115

421559LV00001B/1/P